Dimensions. Journal of Architectural Knowledge
04/2022

Essentials of Montage in Architecture

Issue Editors

Max Treiber, Sandra Meireis, Julian Franke

[transcript]

This journal is published bianually (in spring and autumn) and printed editions are available for annual subscription directly from the publisher. The retail price for an annual subscription to the print issue incl. shipment within Germany is 75,00 € and for international purchases 85,00 €. The electronic version is available free of charge (Open Access).

All information regarding notes for contributors, subscriptions, Open Access, back volume and orders is available online at:
https://www.transcript-publishing.com/dak

Additional information on upcoming issues, calls for contributions and the options for partaking as contributors, editors or members of the peer review procedure can be found at the journals website: www.dimensions-journal.eu
If you have any further questions please contact us, addressing Katharina Voigt, at: mail@dimensions-journal.eu

Bibliographic information published by the Deutsche Nationalbibliothek

The Deutsche Nationalbibliothek lists this publication in the Deutsche National-bibliografie; detailed bibliographic data are available in the Internet at http://dnb.de

Dimensions. Journal of Architectural Knowledge

Lead Editors
Katharina Voigt, Uta Graff, Ferdinand Ludwig

Advisory Board
Isabelle Doucet, Susanne Hauser, Klaske Havik,
Jonathan Michael Hill, Wilfried Kühn, Meike Schalk

Editorial Context
BauHow5
Bartlett University College London, Great Britain
Chalmers University Gothenburg, Sweden
Delft University of Technology, Netherlands
Swiss Federal Institute of Technology Zurich, Switzerland
Technical University of Munich, Germany

Associated Institutions
Royal Technical University of Stockholm, Sweden
Technical University of Vienna, Austria
University of the Arts Berlin, Germany

The initial funding to this journal is provided by the Department of Architecture at the TUM School of Engineering and Design in Munich, Germany.

First published 2023 by transcript Verlag, Bielefeld
© Max Treiber, Sandra Meireis, Julian Franke (eds.)

Cover layout: Katharina Voigt, Technical University of Munich
Copy-editing: Max Treiber, Sandra Meireis, Julian Franke
Proofreading: Lisa Goodrum, London
Typeset: Max Treiber, Technical University of Munich
Printed by Majuskel Medienproduktion GmbH, Wetzlar
ISSN 2747-5085
eISSN 2747-5093
Print-ISBN 978-3-8376-5921-4
PDF-ISBN 978-3-8394-5921-8
HTML-ISBN 978-3-7435-5921-9

Printed on permanent acid-free text paper.

Contents

RECEPTION

PERCEPTION

Contributors

Contents

RECEPTION

PERCEPTION

Contributors

The series *FUTURE MEMORIES, first published in 2021,* explores how our conceptions of the future have changed over the past few decades, how that affects our take on the present and our reactions to changes that lie ahead. Re-created by the artists for the most part out of archival material, the pictures in this issue constitute a material exploration of the fact that every vision or illustration of the future is bound to be a montage of images drawn from the past.

Using a combination of large-format analog photography and various digitally controlled laser technologies, the artists have created a visual world that makes sci-fi allusions and takes an associative approach to an emotional world that swings back and forth between the optimism of the artists' childhood and the dystopianism of the present day and age.

Taiyo Onorato & Nico Krebs

Editorial
Essentials of Montage in Architecture

Max Treiber, Sandra Meireis, Julian Franke

The technique of montage or process of mounting not only led us, as issue editors, to discuss, exchange ideas, and think about the topic of montage in depth as the subject of this publication but it is also a genuine editing technique that helped us to arrange the structure of this issue of *Dimensions. Journal of Architectural Knowledge:* »Essentials of Montage in Architecture«, 04/2022. As fully described in the introductory section, the journal's unique feature is the combination of texts and visual contributions that arose from our call for papers in early December 2021. More precisely, six full texts and three visual contributions handed in by the authors, plus artworks from the series *Future Memories* by the duo Onorato & Krebs were invited by us as an artistic position to accompany the different sections throughout the issue. Together, they form a specific balance of text and image, and help to shape the character of this publication by inviting readers to discover the theme of »Montage in Architecture« in full swing.

A few words on the idea of a visual contribution: Other than a full text paper as the traditional academic and scientific format, a visual contribution focuses on the narrative of the image which is merely accompanied by explanatory text. It is an alternative format that is to be understood as part of the progressive opening and diversification of academic publishing and aims to make previously hidden positions and voices visible and heard.

The idea for the topic *Essentials of Montage in Architecture* derives from Max Treiber's ongoing PhD in the architecture faculty of the Technical University of Munich and his approach can be seen in a contribution to this issue. Sandra Meireis and Julian Franke were invited by Treiber to join the editorial team and they contributed their expertise to the issue additionally with Meireis's historical-theoretical reflection in the introduction and a text focusing on processes of perception by Franke.

Many thanks go to all the published contributors, the reviewers who took part in the peer review process, Taiyo Onorato and Nico Krebs for providing us with their exceptional photomontages, and not least the lead editors of the *Dimensions* journal: Uta Graff, Ferdinand Ludwig, and Katharina Voigt, with the support of the Technical University of Munich. You all contributed to making this journey a very smooth, joyful, and enriching experience for us!

Max Treiber, Sandra Meireis, and Julian Franke

Dimensions. Journal of Architectural Knowledge, 2022-04 ∂
https://doi.org/10.14361/dak-2022-0402

Introduction
Expanding the Notion of Montage in Architecture

Sandra Meireis

Montage is an experimental methodological process and editing technique that comes into use as a creative practice and generates new narrative forms in visual arts, design, and communication. The process is characterized by the appropriation, combination, juxtaposition, and superimposition of heterogeneous sources, both material and immaterial, that are collected, assembled, arranged or inserted as fragments into an existing situation so that *something new* is created. The technique was originally developed in the fields of cinematography, literature, and photography, where it has set strong impulses for new ways of thinking in the early 20th century, such as in the works of the Dadaists and Constructivists. As a multi-sensory cultural technique and playful design methodology, it also became the focus of attention in architecture and urban design, and was adopted in projects such as Yona Friedman's *Ville Spatiale* (an ongoing project starting in 1959), Superstudio's Continuous Monument (1969) or as a theoretical endeavor in Oswald Mathias Ungers's *City Metaphors* (1976/1982). Montages favor contradictory and irritating juxtapositions over a solely aesthetic presentation, which is rather characteristic of collages uniting heterogeneous elements on one level of meaning. Although in both methods of composition, collages and montages, the original properties of mounted fragments remain identifiable, the indexical quality of the imported elements is different. At the montage's heart lies the intellectual process of dialectics, serving didactic purposes, where the viewer takes an active role in the production of (new) meaning. This is where our epistemological interest stems from: Montage is a highly affective and effective medium in architecture and its significance in current architectural discourse should be emphasized and expanded, as will be demonstrated in this issue.

Corresponding author: Sandra Meireis (State Academy of Fine Arts Stuttgart, Germany);
meireis@architekturwissenschaft.net; http://orcid.org/0000-0002-8561-6060

Historically, montage is typically identified as urban, visual, and spatial, as the art historian Martino Stierli explains in his seminal work *Montage and the Metropolis* (2018) where he provides us with:

> »an understanding of montage as a wide-reaching cultural technique that evolved in an increasingly interdisciplinary era, but that is primarily urban in its subject matter and method and that therefore is preoccupied, across media, with coming to an understanding of modern metropolitan space through its architecture« (Stierli 2018: 27).

Here, the technique of montage is a perceptual phenomenon of the modern metropolis in its omnipresent multi-layered urban mobility and it is central to the avant-garde as *the* mode of artistic representation. According to Stierli, five critical features indicate the definition of the urban montage, in short: Montage is defined by the heterogeneity or plurality of the image; montage is a spatial constellation; montage is polyfocal and therefore posits a mobile and embodied viewer; montage is a consequence of industrialization and the age of technological reproducibility; montage is a consequence of the perceptual revolution brought about by the modern metropolis and seeks to visualize an (urban) reality not yet seen (Stierli 2018: 4–16). In this sense, Walter Benjamin's *Arcades Project* (1927–1940) can be understood as a historiographic equivalent, while Le Corbusier's method of comparison in *Vers une architecture* (1923) and Ludwig Mies van der Rohe's early photomontages can be understood as witnesses to this technique in the history of architecture.

For the development of his cinematographic montage theory, the filmmaker Sergei M. Eisenstein describes in his seminal text *Montage and Architecture* (1938) typical »montage structures« in which the perception of space and time is combined in sequential processes. For example, he refers to the architectural historian Auguste Choisy's description of the perception of the Athenian Acropolis while circumnavigating the Parthenon or the depiction of polyfocal pictorial spaces of underground architectural fantasies (*carceri d'invenzione*) by the Renaissance architect Giambattista Piranesi. He also turns his attention to the Catholic Church, especially to the Stations of the Cross, the twelve sculptural groups representing the places that Jesus stopped during his procession to Golgotha. Similarly, he describes a walk around the baldachin by the Baroque sculptor Gian Lorenzo Bernini in St. Peter's, particularly the plinths of its four gigantic columns that are decorated with the eight coats of arms of the Barberini pope. In addition, some of Eisenstein's most famous contemporaries in the architectural field are mentioned because their specific working methods are particularly suited to cinematographic modes of representation, such as Le Corbusier's idea of the *promenade architecturale* and the axonometric drawings by Konstantin Melnikov or the Vkhutemas.

Decades later, the manifesto of media theory avant la lettre, *The Medium is the Massage: An Inventory of Effects* (1967) by Marshall McLuhan, and the hippies' self-published DIY manifestos such as the *Whole Earth Catalog* (since 1968) made use of the montage technique and modeled an alternative graphic art aesthetic and distinctive counterculture work ethic.

Furthermore, this also touches upon issues in the discussion about contemporary architectural research methodologies and the historiography of architecture. Considering the increased interest of architecture researchers in ethnographic and sociological research methods, the work of the anthropologist George E. Marcus is worth mentioning. In *The Modernist Sensibility in Recent Ethnographic Writing and the Cinematic Metaphor of Montage* (1990), Marcus proposes that the montage principle shall be applied to ethnographic writing in order to generate representations that consider the non-linear narration of ethnographic research and daily life. That means when introducing oral history or historical throwbacks to narrative timelines, a montage effect is created that interweaves the past and present and combines the differing views of individuals and academic discourse non-hierarchically.

Generally, the state of the art in media technology has had a great influence on the use of montage. While »photomontage [...] can be seen as a consequence of the development of a modern media society in the early twentieth century« (Stierli 2018: 14), with the rise of social media, montage has gained new momentum due to the development of the late-modern digital society in the early twenty-first century. Today, montage techniques have become an everyday practice for smart phone users, for example, internet memes usually function via amusing juxtapositions of text and image. This also impacts the sphere of architecture, such as on Instagram where The Queer Architect mounts humorous scenes in post-rendering aesthetics to depict the history of architecture in the light of shifting gender norms and roles. Architecture offices such as Lütjens Padmanabhan (Zurich) or Made in (Geneva) also appreciate the technique of montage for its ability to highlight the transition between two or more objects:

»In collage you see breaks. In montage, on the other hand, there are transitions – like in Beethoven; it's not the themes that are important, but the transitions. In montage, you have to work on these. No matter how foreign two objects are to each other: the task of an architect is to bring two or more worlds together. And there are other differences: In collage, you read everything on one level. A montage can be seen as an image on the one hand, but on the other hand it has another level of information. We want to create images – that is, to ensure readability from all sides« (Charbonnet 2017: 31; author's transl.).

Increasingly, fragmentary and disruptive forms of presentation provoke contemporary content, for example the latest developments in artificial intelligence (AI) technology use montage techniques as tools to bring together archived information under certain parameters and create new, albeit questionable, architectural future worlds. These are just a few examples of how montage techniques are used in the field of architecture, in addition to the contributions in this issue that broaden the spectrum as follows.

Structure of the Issue

The selection and compilation of textual and visual contributions address »Essentials of Montage in Architecture« from different perspectives: Theories, methods, and visions highlight the relevance of montage to communicating, designing, perceiving, and reflecting on visual and spatial practices, as well as knowledge production on the discipline of architecture. As editors of this issue, we believe that in the discipline of architecture, especially »the various strands of the meaning of montage — its technological, pictorial, spatial, and epistemological dimensions — are fused together« (Davide Deriu cited after Stierli 2018: 31). Our intention or motivation is to broaden and deepen insight into architectural subjects from an expanded notion of montage in architecture and in this way, we regard the contributions to this issue as laying the foundations for further discussions and research around, and beyond, »Essentials of Montage in Architecture«.

The three sections »Conception, Reception, and Perception« stand for different thematic aspects of the concept of montage in the context of architecture. The word stem -ception derives from the Latin cipere and translates as »to take up/grasp« or »to reassemble from the archives«. Here, we see a central gesture of the montage process as a basis and with the respective prefixes (con-, re-, per-) differentiating assignments are possible.

Conception refers to the traditional understanding of the term montage which is discussed on the basis of the themes: *cinematography, literature,* and *translation*. **Reception** refers to capturing and transforming reality through montage principles. This is discussed on the basis of the themes *experiment, performativity,* and *photography*. **Perception** refers to the recipient's active role in the montage process which is discussed on the basis of the themes: *interpretation, mental montage,* and *phenomenology*. On the one hand, this conceptual triad has resulted from the contributions submitted which we have accordingly allocated by theme; on the other hand, we as editors decided on this triad because we see various perspectives and narratives redeemed here and which offer themselves for further linking and processing. Each contribution is assigned to a specific thematic section, with the inevitable thematic overlaps and uncertainties included and briefly described as follows.

Conception: In the text »Transmission of Knowledge: Eisenstein, Le Corbusier, and Montage as Image Practice in Film and Architecture«, **Ulrike Kuch** highlights the similarities between working with film and architecture that are exemplified in the works of Eisenstein and Le Corbusier, accumulated in their image practices, and whose ideas are linked by the machine (the camera and the house) as an ideological, formal, and aesthetic object. The gaps in a series of images or in the built environment, give rhythm and structure that are perceived as a whole by the moving body and reveal the relevance of time in the understanding of space. **Stefana Dilova**'s visual contribution »Montage of Memories: The Poetics of Home« is based on a self-created cinematographic interpretation of the Japanese novel *Territory of Light* that follows the lives of a single mother and her daughter over the course of a year. The family's apartment is the place where many pivotal moments take place and everyday life is described in a highly poetic style. Dilova combines fictional elements with personal experiences of her time in Japan in a dense atmospheric stop-motion montage technique. In the text »Montaged Gardens – On Paper: The *Red Books* by Landscape Designer Humphry Repton«, **Achim Reese** analyzes the *Red Books* as functioning as representational instruments to convey Humphry Repton's ideas for improved garden designs. Repton primarily operated as a consultant in the 18th century. The flaps can be read as a montage technique where two identical states are juxtaposed and create an illusion of movement in space and time; from the original to the improved, thus illuminating the difference between the old and the new.

Reception: Max Treiber's contribution »Realmontage: Photographic Readings of Everyday Spaces« reflects a series of seminars held at Technical University of Munich that dealt with spatial investigations through photography and which resulted in translations for architectural design. The investigations aimed to expand the students' understanding of the built environment and broaden the spectrum of their design methods. In the visual contribution »Montage: From Images to Narratives« **Erieta Attali** examines her own long-standing artistic photographic practice, focusing on architecture from multiple standpoints within the landscape. Layered transparent and reflective surfaces contribute to her approach of creating architectural walks or paths through nature by making use of image sequences that mount temporal and spatial impressions into new environmental narratives or hybrid realities. In the text »Artistic Practice as Preservation Process: The Performative Potential of Montage«, **Katrine Majlund Jensen** advocates for an expanded notion of preservation as a creative rather than a restorative field of practice, as exemplified in Alex Lehnerer's and Savvas Ciriacidis's spatial montage *Bungalow Germania* which was exhibited at the Venice Architecture Biennale in 2014. Experimental preservation is regarded as a chance to widen the conventional frames and process of operational doubt.

Perception: Julian Franke describes processes of human perception in the text »Montages in Mind: On the Formative Role of Perceivers in Architecture« and reveals striking parallels with montaging as an artistic editing technique. Perceiving includes, besides the senses, the imaginative juxtaposition and superimposition of individual experiences, memories, desires, and expectations as a basis for the subjective and intersubjective construction of the built environment and world. In the visual contribution »Qualities of Space: Montage within Painting and Architecture«, **Nils Fröhling** tests the hypothesis that human spatial perception has changed with new media technologies and means of transportation. Boundaries dissolve and everyday dichotomies, such as private and public sphere, interior and exterior space, real and virtual events, collapse into an imaginary stream of accelerated travel through the urban space. Fröhling processes these observations in a series of photorealistic digital paintings that can be described as montages of contemporary spatial phenomena. In the text »Mind the Gaps: Brutalism, Montage, and Parkour«, **Charles Engle** highlights the particular movement and potential of *parkour* through the built environment as a montage technique that is intrinsic to this particular subcultural scene which combines the street with media practices and where architecture, the body, and politics confront each other in performative sequences.

In the selection and compilation of textual and visual contributions according to the thematic triad: »conception, reception, perception« we ensured that content and form came together in a comprehensive way to relate all of these diverse perspectives and narratives of montage to each other, while also roaming through the issue.

References

Beitin, Andreas/Eiermann, Wolf/Franzen, Brigitte (eds.) (2017): *Ludwig Mies van der Rohe: Montage, Collage.* Exhibition catalog. Ludwig Forum Aachen and Museum Georg Schäfer Schweinfurt, London: Koenig Books.

Benjamin, Walter (2002): *The Arcades Project,* edited by Rolf Tiedemann, transl. by Howard Eiland and Kevin McLaughlin, Cambridge, MA: Belknap Press.

Charbonnet, François (2017): »Die Kraft des Fragments« (»The Power of the Fragment«); Oliver Lütjens and Thomas Padmanabhan in conversation with François Charbonnet, in: *Archithese* 3, 28–37.

Eisenstein, Sergei M. (1989 [1937–1940]): »Montage and Architecture«, transl. by Michael Glenny, in: *Assemblage 10,* 110–131, http://www.jstor.org/stable/3171145, accessed July 15, 2022.

Le Corbusier (2008 [1924]): *Toward an Architecture [Vers une architecture],* edited by Jean-Louis Cohen, transl. by John Goodman, London: Lincoln.

Marcus, George E. (1990): »The Modernist Sensibility in Recent Ethnographic Writing and the Cinematic Metaphor of Montage«, in: *Visual Anthropology Review 6 (1),* 2–12, doi: 10.1525/var.1990.6.1.2

McLuhan, Marshall/Fiore, Quentin (1967): *The Medium is the Massage: An Inventory of Effects,* Corte Madera, CA: Gingko Press.

Stierli, Martino (2018): *Montage and the Metropolis: Architecture, Modernity, and the Representation of Space,* New Haven, CT: Yale University Press.

CONCEPTION

»The discursive element of the montage in interrupting established order leaves us with the question of what meaning architecture holds when its functions and embedded metaphors are disturbed.«

Katrine Majlund Jensen: *Artistic Practice as Preservation Process, p. 161.*

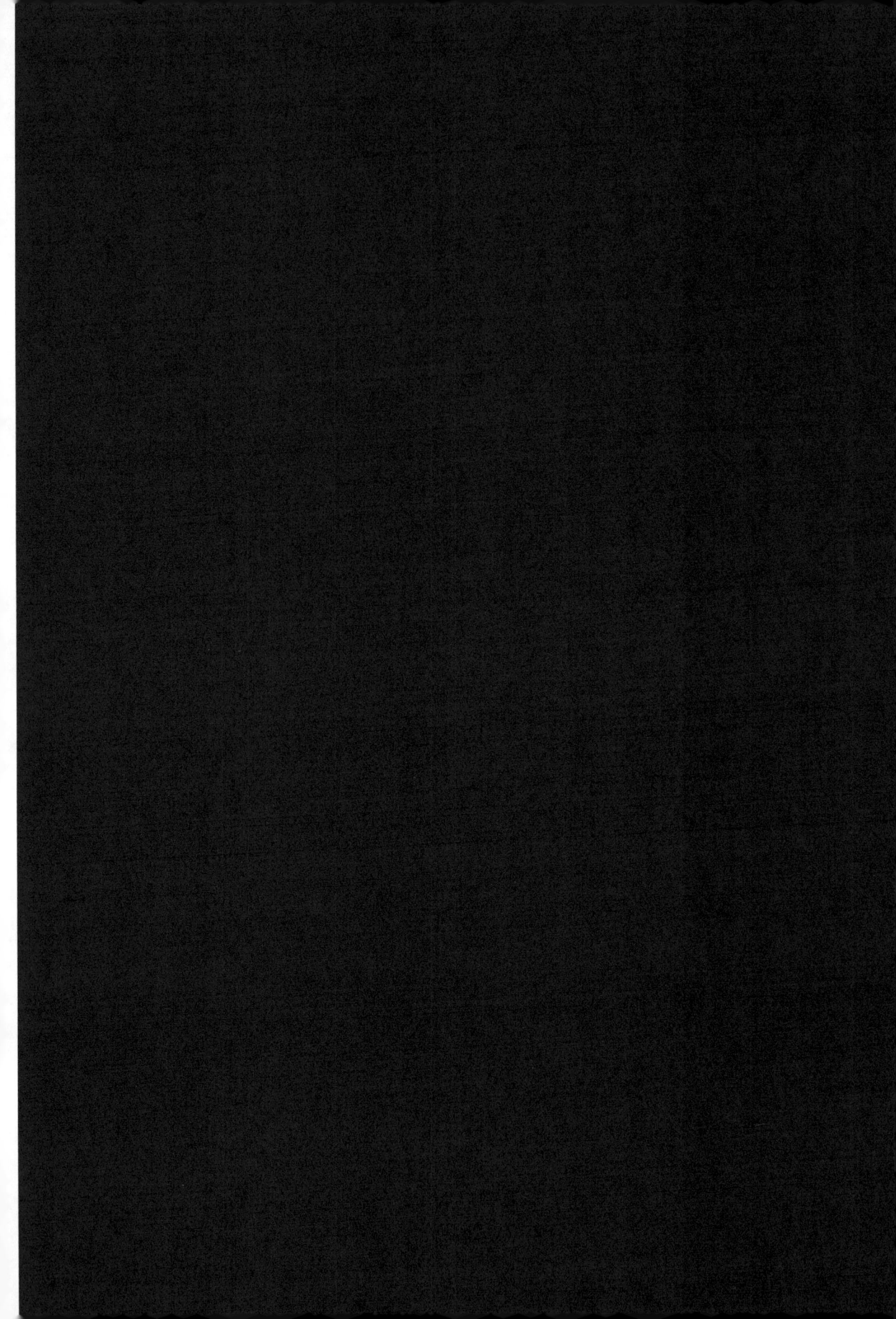

Dimensions. Journal of Architectural Knowledge, 2022-04 ⮌
https://doi.org/10.14361/dak-2022-0404

Transmission of Knowledge
Eisenstein, Le Corbusier, and Montage as Image Practice in Film and Architecture

Ulrike Kuch

Abstract: There are many ways to gain knowledge about architecture: sensing, drawing, building, and thinking for example. When thinking about architecture, leaving the interior point of view and looking from the outside toward architecture offers a broad variety of perspectives. This helps us to understand, moreover to develop different design approaches for architectures: Looking from the outside, architectural design implies a certain attitude toward the world. Using a film lense for this look, I will reveal the relevance of cinematic techniques.

Thus, in this article I suggest switching to film theory and history. With the help of director Sergei Eisenstein and architect Le Corbusier we will explore how architecture and film share an intensive relationship with images. If we take a closer look, we will see that montage as a cinematic technique to attach images reveals characteristics of architecture that we might not have been aware of – the relevance of gaps, for example. Thus, images are entities with which to transmit knowledge from film to architecture and back, while montage is the practice of working with images and their inherent knowledge. Accordingly, this article aims to analyze how montage is used as image practice in the work of Eisenstein and Le Corbusier.

Keywords: 1920s Avantgarde; Eisenstein; Imageness; Le Corbusier; Phenomenology.

Corresponding author: Ulrike Kuch (Bauhaus University Weimar, Germany);
ulrike.kuch@uni-weimar.de; https://orcid.org/0000-0003-1318-573X

Introduction

When one thinks of architecture, one probably thinks of space first; which of course is right but we might also think of images: images in our mind's eye, and perhaps even images recorded by our body – images of space that we experienced through our moving bodies.

Cinema is the place for such experiences. Through the eye of the camera, we – our flesh and mind, phenomenologically speaking: our *Leib*, here translated as body – experience architectural spaces in moving images. In cinema however, it is not *our* body that is moving, but the pictures, the camera, and sometimes, also another being on the screen. Without our perceiving body, without the memories of movement stored in our body, the immersive experience of *cinematographic space* – as I would like to term this in-between space, this dialogic mechanism – would not work. Think, for example, of the terrifying rising up of the streets in Inception (Nolan 2010) or the impression of being hopelessly lost in the labyrinthine staircase in *The Name of the Rose* (Jean-Jacques Annaud 1986). The (spatial) relationship of the perceiving body and the space and body on the screen characterizes the cinematographic space. Using this concept it is possible to analyze and evaluate how architecture in film relates to the perceiver and their spatial perception (cf. Kuch 2013: 3–9). I will therefore return to this concept when we take a closer look at Eisenstein's films.

Architecture and space, images, movement, and the body are deeply connected; and so are architecture and film. In the following text I will look at architecture through film and through images in motion to see what happens to architecture as our understanding of *image* as a phenomenological-anthropological term changes. In turn, I will also look at what happens to our understanding of the image, when we consider the relationship between image and architecture, which in English might be termed imageness.

More precisely, I suggest viewing montage as image practice in the work of Eisenstein and Le Corbusier. For both artists, the selection, composition, and arrangement of images follow a respective artistic approach that they developed in a process of mutual reflection. For architects today, these observations might help to develop a different view of architecture, especially in terms of the relationship between the perceiving person, the act of perception and the spatial organization of architecture. Simultaneously, we will travel through 1920s Europe, from Moscow to Paris via Hamburg and La Sarraz.

Le Corbusier and the Russian film avantgarde

In 1928, Le Corbusier visited Moscow for the first time (cf. the fundamental and groundbreaking work by Jean-Luis Cohen, 1987). At a time when Hitler and the Nazis were growing increasingly strong, the Russian state was seen by many communist sympathizers as a country with a brilliant future. To architects it was especially attractive: it had a growing artistic avant-garde in many fields and it was forging a new vision for society, building a new state, and with it, a new economic reality. When he arrived, Le Corbusier was already a well-known and notable architect in Russia. He visited several buildings and appreciated the architectural quality he saw. In the years that followed, he went on to design and build two important buildings, and even dreamed of realizing his ideas for reorganizing Moscow. Yet, as the Russian government turned increasingly toward neo-classical architecture, Le Corbusier's relationship with Russia came to an end, most obviously with the 1932 rejection of his exceptional entry to the Palace of the Soviets competition.

On his first trip in 1928 Le Corbusier was warmly welcomed and was introduced to the who's who of the Russian architectural elite, among them Sergei Michailowitsch Eisenstein. During his visit, he attended a screening of Eisenstein's films *Bronenosets Patyomkin* (*Battleship Potemkin* [1925]) and *Generalnaja Linja* (*The General Line* [1927], also known as: *Staroye i novoye/ Old and New* [1929]). Upon leaving, Le Corbusier gave Eisenstein a copy of *L'art decoratif d'aujourd'hui* from 1925, which included his essay »Esprit de verité«, which I will discuss later. The dedication is quite remarkable:

> »To M. Eisenstein this dedication after Potemkin and The Straight Line [sic].
> I seem to think as M. Eisenstein does when he makes films. Spirit of truth, a coat of whitewash, two chapters that express the same conviction. With my deepest sympathy and highest regard« (Cohen 1987: 49).

Eisenstein and Le Corbusier admired their work – still, it was not a deep friendship that united them, but the mutual inspiration throughout the works can be traced throughout their oeuvres.

»Esprit de verité«, in English »Spirit of truth«, highlights Le Corbusier's search for intensity and truth in architecture. An important inspiration for Le Corbusier was Dziga Vertov who, in his essay »Kino-Glaz« (»Cine-Eye«) (1919) and his film *The Man with the Movie Camera* (1929), identified the camera as an observer and the unique technique of truth. Vertov, one the protagonists of early film and film theory, moves the camera/observer and melts the body, eye, and apparatus within the moving image. Vertov's explanation expresses the crux of his attempt, it concludes subjectivity as well as objectivity:

> »I am kino-eye, I am a mechanical eye. I, a machine, show you the world as only I can see it.
>
> Now and forever, I free myself from human immobility, I am in constant motion, I draw near, then away from objects, I crawl under, I climb onto them. I move apace with the muzzle of a galloping horse, I plunge full speed into a crowd, I outstrip running soldiers, I fall on my back, I ascend with an airplane. I plunge and soar together with plunging and soaring bodies. Now I, a camera, fling myself along their resultant, maneuvering in the chaos of movement, recording movement, starting with movements composed of the most complex combinations.
>
> Freed from the rule of sixteen – seventeen frames per second, free of the limits of time and space, I put together any given points in the universe, no matter where I've recorded them. My path leads to the creation of a fresh perception of the world. I decipher in a new way a world unknown to you« (Vertov 1923: 17f).

This sets the tone for the Russian way of experimenting with cinematography. In a similar manner, Le Corbusier describes cinema as a machine for revealing »the truth«:

> »Therefore, it's necessary to conceive and then to see. It's necessary to have the *notion* of vision. [...] The base [of cinema, author's addition] is the apparatus of physics, the lens of the camera – as eye. [...] But I want the lens now to disclose the intensity of human consciousness to us through the intermediary of visual phenomena which are so subtle and so rapid in nature that we are [...] unable to observe them [...]. I say, therefore, that the nerveless, soulless lens is a prodigious voyeur, a discoverer, a revealer, a proclaimer. And through it, we can enter into the truth of human consciousness« (Le Corbusier 1933: 111ff [original emphasis]).

Moreover, the camera is a neutral and unerring tool to train perception, making the viewer conscious of what is relevant for architecture. For Le Corbusier, this meant proportions, harmony, rhythm, relationship to nature, and to man. He saw the same intention in Eisenstein's work, elaborating on it in an interview a few weeks later:

>>Architecture and cinema are the only two arts of our time. In my own work I seem to think as Eisenstein does in his films. His work is shot through with the sense of truth, and bears witness to the truth alone. In their ideas, his films resemble closely what I am striving to do in my own work<< (Le Corbusier, quoted in Cohen 1987: 49).

Even though we know that Le Corbusier was a master of self-promotion and a man with a large ego not afraid of opportunism, his comments in the Russian interview are extraordinary. So what was it that struck Le Corbusier's attention?

When we watch the cream separator sequence of *Generalnaja linja* (fig. 1), we are watching Eisenstein's theory of montage. In contrast to Vertov, for Eisenstein films are artworks, he tried to combine images to get a harsh effect. Here, the rhythm of the images, the combination of the machine, human beings, milk, of dark and light, of abstract and concrete images, of different materials and surfaces, of anger, sadness, and happiness effects an intensity that Eisenstein is renowned for. His aim was to combine images in a way that in their sum told more than a usual sequence of images ever could. He wanted to create a feeling of ecstasy and pathos. Eisenstein chose images with a deep psychological impact: close-up shots that heightened the intensity of it. The machine, like the cream separator in this sequence, was his favorite aesthetic object, a source of light effects and abstract images that symbolize futurism and progress. This handling of images – montage and the use of intensive abstract and futuristic images – is unique and links his films to other avant-garde art films by Hans Richter, László Moholy-Nagy or Man Ray, and this was the aspect where he saw a close connection to architecture, as we will see later.

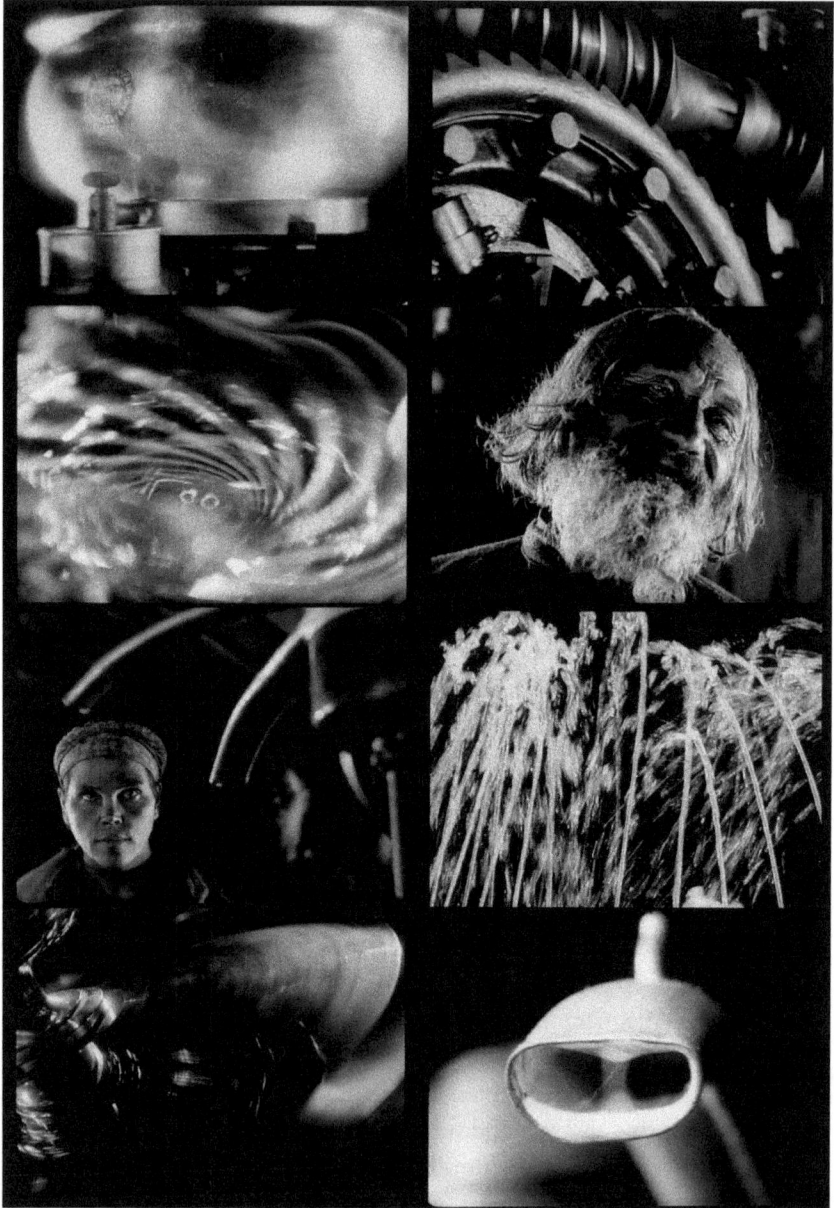

1.
*Cream separator sequence as an example of the configuration of abstract and
concrete images in Eisenstein's films, UdSSR, 1926.*
Photographs: Sergei Eisenstein.

In the cream separator sequence, Eisenstein »raises the everyday events that escape our superficial attention [...] to the level of monumental images« (ibid.), states Le Corbusier. We know that Le Corbusier compared his designs with machines, writing in his famous *Vers une architecture/ Towards a New Architecture* in 1923/1931: »A house is a machine for living-in« (Le Corbusier 1923/1927: 95). In *Generalnaja linja* the two came together: the machine links the ideas of Eisenstein and Le Corbusier as ideological, formal and aesthetic object. Thus, even if the artistic expression in terms of the handling of the image differs, the fascination of the camera as a machine to »reveal the truth« strikes both.

Film and Architecture, Architecture and Film – Eisenstein and Sequences of Images

Eisenstein was himself very fond of architecture. He was trained as a civil engineer in Saint Petersburg and carefully followed the architectural debate on modernism in Russia. Architecture was first and foremost an important inspiration for him. He made sketches for several projects, including, for example, *The Glass House* project, a critical consideration of recent ideas by Bruno Taut, Paul Scheerbart, and Le Corbusier (Bulgakowa 1966). Eisenstein was especially interested in the physical and psychological features of glass. In his project sketch, he imagined the stacking of transparent rooms. Thus, Eisenstein critically commented on the psychological pressure of private and public surveillance. As Oksana Bulgakowa has noted, he also cut out images of glass skyscrapers from newspaper articles (comparing them to the architecture of *Metropolis* by Fritz Lang [1927]; Bulgakowa 1966: 113). We can see the influence of this architectural discourse in *Generalnaja Linja*, where he shows a bright white cubic diary with longitudinal windows, a flat roof and thin columns (cf. Vidler 2019).

Moreover, Eisenstein founded his montage theory on images of architecture. In conjunction with ecstasy, for example, he referred to Piranesi and, remarkably, also to Auguste Choisy. Like Le Corbusier – perhaps because he owned a copy of *Vers une architecture* –Eisenstein admired Choisy's description of the Acropolis in Athens from 1899 (Cohen 1987; cf. Kuch 2013: 173–177; Vidler 2019). He read it as a sequence of images that could be perceived by a moving body – as a »cinematographic space« avant la lettre. Choisy writes:

»Ainsi se sont succédé trois tableaux correspondant à trois point de vue prin-
cipaux [...]. Et dans chacun d'eux un seul monument a dominé [...] : cette unité
du motif principal assurait la simplicité de l'impression, l'unité du tableau. [...]
Chaque motif d'architecture pris à part est symétrique, mais chaque groupe
est traité comme un paysage où les masses seules se pondèrent. [...] Si main-
tenant nous parcourons la série des tableaux que l'Acropole nous a offerts,
sans exception nous les trouverons combinés en vue de la première impression« (Choisy 1964 [1899]: 333).

Choisy inspired Le Corbusier's idea of the *promenade architecturale* – of
different views on architecture perceived by the moving body. Thus, both
Eisenstein and Le Corbusier refer to the same source for their idea of creating
sequences of images in film and architecture. Additionally, Eisenstein wrote
an article titled »Synchronization of Senses« that undertook an in-depth
discussion of music, rhythm and motion, perspective, and the juxtaposition
of images (Eisenstein 1928). In this article, Eisenstein compares his montage
theory and jazz. He especially quotes an architectural metaphor – stairs – to
describe the development of film (ibid.: 97). This would be another fruitful
perspective and possible knowledge transmission. I will stick to our framework for now, though.

Through his understanding of images detached from their representative character and replaced by a sequence of images that work together to
create a montage, Eisenstein stands alongside two other contemporaries:
Fritz Schumacher and Aby Warburg. Schumacher, an architect in Hamburg,
speaking of architecture, said that: »Bewegung und Bild zeitigen etwas
neues« (»movement and image yield something new«) (Schumacher 1983
[1938]: 227), while Warburg, a famous art historian and friend of Schumacher,
arranged the heterogenous images of his *Mnemosyne-Atlas* as a sequence
of similar reproductions on black canvas and undertook research on these
images on movements stored in gestures. For him, as for Eisenstein, and
in the 1940s for philosopher Maurice Merleau-Ponty, the intersection, the
interval, or the crack was the most fascinating. According to Philippe-Alain
Michaud, »only the insertion in a sequence of images transforms them into
unities of expression« (Michaud 2007: 283; cf. Merleau-Ponty 2016 [1964]).
Furthermore, the in-between, one of the most important aspects of phenomenology, can also be found in-between the images. Elena Vogman analyzes
Eisenstein's thinking about the tension, collision, and motion of images, and
in-between images, and points out that rhythm depends on these elements
(Vogman 2018: 438–444).

Eisenstein uses similar terms (*pathos formula*) and similar models of thought (pendulum) as Warburg. For both, motion and dynamics are core elements of art. These ideas link Warburg, the phenomenologist Maurice Merleau-Ponty, and Eisenstein most significantly: The series of images with in-between-gaps is becoming a movie through motion. In cinema, it is the motion of the film strip that produces movements, it is the montage of images that produces emotions, in Warburg's *Mnemosyne- Atlas* it is the spectator who(se eye) moves. Montage, in this sense, does not mean hiding the gaps between the images, but more than that, accepting it as an important and consciously used factor within a series of images that, in their arrangement, create tension. Through motion, the series of images are perceived as a whole; as a film sequence.

Thinking of architecture, this aspect of montage is immediately convincing: Gaps understood as joints between different building components are substantial for creating architecture. Looking at montage, its potential as *fugue* comes to the fore: Gaps structure architectural arrangements, they bring in rhythm, and complete the architectural image. An almost banal example are the gaps and holes on exposed concrete walls, resulting from the construction panels, such as in Tadao Ando's works. Just as in Otto Wagner's Postsparkassenamt, those gaps and holes become ornaments, in the sense that they are part of a composition and carefully arranged. Through fugues, Wagner's and Ando's architectural images are completed.

Moreover, gaps as a distinctive interruption between images in architecture can be seen in the Jewish Museum in Berlin by Daniel Libeskind. Here, the *mise en scène* of the architectural images, characterized by the gaps, evoke strong emotions that are comparable to what Eisenstein aimed for. Another, more artistic example of the skilful and artistic use of gaps is Gordon Matta-Clark's *Cuttings*. The whole process of producing a gap, a hole or even dividing a house, involves several of the aforementioned aspects, such as relation to time, the evocation of strong feelings, and finally, creating strong architectural images.

Le Corbusier and the Camera as Perceiving Machine

Le Corbusier's views on film and architecture, and maybe also on Eisenstein's movies, are reflected in the short film *L'architecture d'aujourd'hui* from 1930. To understand the emergence of this film, we revisit the Parisian avant-garde of the late 1920s, of which Le Corbusier was a part and which had a strong connection to Eisenstein: Right before, in 1928, the Congres International d'Architecture Moderne (CIAM) held a conference at the castle La Sarraz in Switzerland, near Lausanne. The meeting was initiated by Le Corbusier, and attended by his very prominent contemporaries, including Walter Gropius, Sigfried Giedion, and Hans Richter. One year later, in 1929, Hélène de Mandrot welcomed the Congres International du Cinema Independent (CICI) to her castle. Just like one year before, the avant-garde accepted the invitation: among others, Sergei Eisenstein, Alberto Cavalcanti, Leon Moussinac, Walter Ruttmann, Hans Richter (again!), and Béla Balász discussed the emergence of film at La Sarraz.

At that time, Paris was the home of film and film theory. Some of the most inspiring directors and most important theorists congregated in Paris to discuss the artistic development of film and its techniques – the close-up, color, and especially sound. Along with Jean Epstein and Leon Moussinac, one of Le Corbusier's friends was Elie Faure, an art historian who worked in different fields. His article »De la cinéplastique« gives us an idea of the discourse on avant-garde film in the late 1920s. Furthermore, Faure outlines how knowledge can emerge in-between the arts. He describes the relationship between film and architecture as a synthesis, which in cinema allows the artist to create an architecture that consists of »tone and modelling« (Faure 1922: 266). He traces this back to the relevance of time in the understanding of space.

The strong connection between architecture and film is made particularly apparent by the photographer and film-maker Man Ray in his film *Les mystères du chateau de Dé* (1929), shot at the Villa Noailles in Hyères. In *Les mystères du chateau de Dé* there is a narrative following the movement of two imaginary visitors to, and through, the Villa Noailles. And it is a journey that explores the highly modern architecture of Robert Mallet-Stevens, who was also a set-designer. The camera is used as an explorer that moves visibly through the building and echoes Le Corbusier's ideal of the camera as a perceiving machine, as he describes it in »Esprit de verité«.

In Paris in the 1920s, avant-garde film theory and avant-garde architecture were as strongly interwoven as possible, and Le Corbusier was receptive to the artistic potential that unfolded in front of his eyes.

In late 1929, the magazine *L'architecture d'aujourd'hui* was founded. It aimed to promote French modern architecture, but also the magazine itself, and to this end, Pierre Chenal was commissioned to produce a film. Le Corbusier, whose architecture played a central role in the film, tried hard to influence Chenal. I mentioned Le Corbusier's ego earlier, and it seems that he was quite successful. The »truth« that Le Corbusier had called for, with a side glance at Eisenstein and Vertov, was now put into practice. The film asks us to see if we can find »truth« anywhere.

In *L'architecture d'aujourd'hui* (fig. 2.), we can see the building from outside, linked to the inside through window-shots, and we see the camera pan horizontally and follow ways into the building and around the outside. »The camera angles suggest a sequence of sunny spaces, each leading on from one to the other, which are stitched together by the movements of the body« writes Flora Samuel (2010: 126).

2.
Le Corbusier: Villa Savoye, 1928–1931, »Une rampe en pente douce conduit au solarium.« Sequence from L'architecture d'aujourd'hui – a smooth journey through Villa Savoye in Poissy, 1930.

We see moving bodies – particularly a young woman – exploring the architectural space for us, and demonstrating what Le Corbusier has created as *promenade architecturale*. While the camera remains fixed on certain viewpoints and just pans slightly, the woman moves swiftly and steadily from the bottom to the top of the house. The moving body as the related object of our perception lets us think ourselves inside the image. We don't need to move, she does, and the architecture pushes her to do so. The process of perception is therefore not a one-way act but a communicative exchange between the viewer and the screen, just as movement in architecture is not just dependent on the moving person, but also on invitations made by the house. *L'architecture d'aujourd'hui* emphasizes this process of perception of architecture champs and hors-champs, inside and outside of the screen and the cinema. Following what we have heard from Le Corbusier's experiences with Vertov and Eisenstein, and with the avant-garde in France, montage here is not the practice of working and thinking with images – a »modus operandi« as Deriu (2007: 57) calls it – the »stitching together« (Samuel) of architecture and images, and of the images themselves. The spatial construction can therefore be regarded as a compelling example of the construction of an architecture-based cinematographic space. In contrast to Eisenstein, montage in this case is not a collision of strong abstract and concrete images to create an emotional effect, but the careful production of depth and a sense of space with a moving body, a creation of architecture in motion.

Following their artistic approach, Chenal and Le Corbusier recall a reduced and ocean steamer-like atmosphere – the house is a machine to live in. However, rhythm as smooth movement plays the central role and thus, montage as image practice is the tool to achieve it.

The Imageness of Architecture

Even if the film is quite short, it effectively conveys the idea of an architecture in motion. As we heard at the beginning, according to Le Corbusier, cinema should reveal the truth. Images link architecture and the viewer through motion and movements, and this is what is so simple and compelling in this sequence.

While Eisenstein's endeavors in montage theory differ considerably from the smooth travelings that we can see in Le Corbusier's movie, the intention – to affect and involve the viewer – is the same. Each in their own way succeeds in carefully composing the *cinematographic space*, a space that stretches between the viewer and the screen, and that involves the body and cinematic architecture in motion. And here we are coming back to the gaps and the in-between of images: For Eisenstein, the gap was the most productive part of films. His ideas of montage all deal with the gap. He thought about the different directions of the moving images and thought of different ways to arrange images. Due to his political and aesthetic impact, his aim was the explosion and collision of images – that is what happens within the cream separator sequence. Le Corbusier's main concern was the presentation of his architectural ideas, and montage was the technique to arrange images on this behalf, a practice of working and thinking with images. Yet both protagonists use the image as a link to the recipient and both use the arrangement of images to create rhythm within their works. Besides the image itself, the medium to transfer these ideas is the body. Thus, montage for Eisenstein is an artistic and intellectual practice within his cinematographic cosmos, while for Le Corbusier, it is an incentive to »reveal the truth« of his architecture.

The idea of an image that is no longer solely representative, but serves as a medium linking architecture, the viewer, and motion is the reason to think about this topic today. The German philosopher Lambert Wiesing, whose work on the phenomenological understanding of images is outstanding, might clarify why these considerations are still relevant. In his work, Wiesing outlines architecture's unique position in the context of image theory. With the term »*artifizielle Präsenz*« (artificial presence), he describes the in-between existence of architecture on screen as something not physical but still existent (Wiesing 2005).

In our context, the imageness of architecture indicates the difference between architecture in reality and architecture on screen, and points to the volatility of the architectural image – and maybe also of architecture itself. This also tells us that »non-real« architecture reveals a presence that is close to the »real« presence of architecture: We can take it seriously.

While in cinema the human body is not always visible, through the camera's movement, and especially in what I call the *morphanthropic* forms of architecture, we notice the human body due to our own experience. With Lambert Wiesing in our mind we can transmit this knowledge from film to architecture: The moving image and the recipients are intersected with the perceiving body – in film and in architecture. The image exists in a process of perception of percipient (and his body) and perceived object.

Architecture itself owns all the significant features of this process. The perception of architecture and the perception of images are thus not contradictory. They need to be understood as two sides of the same coin – a coin that I call the *imageness* of architecture. A paradigmatic example of the cinematic perception of architecture by a moving body is Adolf Loos' Villa Müller in Prague. The arrangement of spaces, stairs, and views generates a carefully arranged sequence of images which can also be termed »montage« (cf. Kuch 2017).

Conclusion

We are affected by the filmic experience. Our body notices the spatial explorations of the camera. The emerging imageness of architecture has an »artificial presence« and does not depend on the canvas or screen. Architecture is an image in motion that refers to the body, to the qualities of architecture, and to space.

The films of Eisenstein and Le Corbusier show how cinematic practices like montage can be used as a medium of architectural experience. The tacit knowledge of architecture – as the example of Eisenstein showed – can be perceived much more intensively in cinema than in reality.

There are several elements that link Eisenstein and Le Corbusier; the most powerful one is the machine. As an apparatus, the machine is relevant to the artistic process either as a camera or house, but also as a reference point for the perception of images and architectures– ideological, future-oriented – meaning. Montage is indeed a term that is very close to these ideas as it expresses a technique as well as a theory: Montage is a practice of working and thinking with images. The gap between images that is so relevant to the idea of montage creates a tension that can be found in architecture and the arts in general (cp. Warburg and Tadao Ando's work, where gaps are fundamental elements of the architectural design). Just like it is described by Flora Samuel with a view to Le Corbusier's film, »spaces [...] are stitched together by the movements of the body«. Motion is an important factor in this context – again in two-sided: as motion of the images and as motion within the images, in the context of montage it is especially apparent as rhythm.

We also observe this in Adolf Loos' Villa Müller or in Rem Koolhaas's Dutch embassy in Berlin. Montage is thus an outstanding example of the transmission of knowledge of architecture and film.

Le Corbusier showed a way to transmit this knowledge between different media. Through his ideas we are aware of the potential of the mutual exploration of film and architecture, as in the *promenade architecturale*, but also in Eisenstein's relationship to Choisy's, Piranesi's and Warburg's intellectual realm. To sum this up: Cinema opens up a different point of view, toward a phenomenological-anthropological understanding of architecture and the image. The potential of this viewpoint can also be observed in other architectural examples. Yet, there is a chance, or maybe a challenge, for today's architects to get even more out of the film-architecture relationship.

References

Bois, Yve-Alain (1989): »Introduction to Eisenstein's ›Montage and Architecture‹«, in: *Assemblage 10*, 112-113.

Bulgakowa, Oksana (1966): *Sergei Eisenstein – drei Utopien: Architekturentwürfe zur Filmtheorie (Sergei Eisenstein – Three Utopias: Architectural Drafts for a Film Theory)*, Berlin: Potemkin Press.

Choisy, Auguste (1964 [1899]): *Histoire de l'architecture, vol. 1*, Paris: Éditions Vincent, Fréal & Cie.

Cohen, Jean-Louis (1987): *Le Corbusier and the Mystique of the USSR: Theories and Projects for Moscow 1928–1936*, Princeton, NJ: Princeton University Press.

Deriu, Davide (2007): »Montage and Modern Architecture: Giedion's Implicit Manifesto«, in: *Architectural Theory Review*, 12/1, 36–59, doi:10.1080/13264820701553096

Eisenstein, Sergei M. (1989 [1937–1940]): »Montage and Architecture«, transl. by Michael Glenny, in: *Assemblage 10*, 111–131.

Eisenstein, Sergei M. (1928): »Synchronization of Senses«, in: Sergei M. Eisenstein, *The Film Sense*, edited by Jay Leyda, New York: Harcourt Brace, 1975, 69–109.

Eisenstein, Sergei M. (1975 [1942]): *The Film Sense*, edited by Jay Leyda, New York: Harcourt Brace.

Eisenstein, Sergei M. (1977): *Über Kunst und Künstler: Über El Greco; Gotik; Piranesi; Wagner; Puschkin (About Art and Artists: About El Greco; Gothic; Piranesi; Wagner; Puschkin)*, transl. by Alexander Kaempfe, München: Rogner and Bernhard.

Faure, Elie (1922): »De la cinéplastique«, in: L'Herbier, Marcel (ed.), *L'Intelligence du cinématographe*, Paris: Editions d'aujourd'hui, 1946/1977, 266–278. – English translation: »The Art of Cineplastics«, in: Abel, Richard (ed.), *French Film Theory and Criticism: A History/ Anthology 1907–1939*, vol. 1 (1907–1929), Princeton, NJ: Princeton University Press, 1988, 258–268.

Kuch, Ulrike (2013): *Die Treppe im Film (The Stairs in the Film)*, unpublished doctoral dissertation, Weimar: The Bauhaus University.

Kuch, Ulrike (2017): »Zwischenraum, Leib, Chronotopos: Das Erscheinen von Zeit auf der Treppe des Films« (»In-between Space, Body, Chronotopos: The Appearance of Time on the Stairs in the Film«), in: Johannes Binotto (ed.), *Film/Architektur: Perspektiven des Kinos auf den Raum (Film/Architecture: Perspectives of the Cinema on Space)*, Bauwelt Fundamente, Berlin: Birkhäuser/De Gruyter, 44-59.

Le Corbusier (1933): »Spirit of truth«, in: Richard Abel (ed.), *French Film Theory and Criticism: A History/Anthology 1907–1939, vol. 2 (1929–1939)*, Princeton, NJ: Princeton University Press, 1988, 111–114.

Le Corbusier (1923): *Vers une architecture. –* English translation by Frederick Etchells: *Towards a New Architecture*, transl. from the thirteenth French edition, London: John Rodker, 1927, repr. Oxford: Architectural Press, 1985.

Merleau-Ponty, Maurice (2016 [1964]): *Le visible et l'invisible: Suivi de notes de travail*, Paris: Gallimard. – English translation: Claude Lefort (ed.): *The Visible and the Invisible. Followed by Working Notes*, transl. by Alphonso Lingis, Evanston, IL: Northwestern University Press, 1968.

Michaud, Philippe-Alain (2007): *Aby Warburg and the Image in Motion*, New York: Zone Books.

Samuel, Flora (2010): *Le Corbusier and the Architectural Promenade*, Basel: Birkhäuser.

Schumacher, Fritz (1983 [1938]): *Der Geist der Baukunst (The Spirit of Architecture)*, Stuttgart: Deutsche Verlags-Anstalt

Vertov, Dziga (1923): »Kinoks: A Revolution« (reprinted from the *Journal of the Left Front of the Arts, no. 3*), in: Vertov, Dziga (1994 [1984]): *Kino-eye: The writings of Dziga Vertov*, edited by Annette Michelson/Kevin O'Brien, Berkeley: University of California Press, 11–21.

Vidler, Anthony (2019): »The Eisenstein Effect: Architecture and Narrative Montage in Sergei Eisenstein and Le Corbusier«, in: Dimendberg, Edward (ed.), *The Moving Eye: Film, Television, Visual Art, and the Modern*, Oxford: Oxford University Press, 57–76, doi10.1093/oso/9780190218430.003.0005

Vogman, Elena (2018): *Sinnliches Denken: Eisensteins exzentrische Methode (Sensuous Thinking: Eisenstein's Eccentric Method)*, Zürich: Diaphanes.

Wiesing, Lambert (2005): *Artifizielle Präsenz: Studien zur Philosophie des Bildes*, Frankfurt a. M.: Suhrkamp. – English translation: *Artificial Presence: Philosophical Studies in Image Theory*, transl. by Nils F. Schott, Stanford: Stanford University Press, 2010.

1.
The staircase, Film still.
Photograph: Stefana Dilova, 2020–2021.

Dimensions. Journal of Architectural Knowledge, 2022-04 ᛞ
https://doi.org/10.14361/dak-2022-0405

Montage of Memories
Poetics of Home

Stefana Dilova

Abstract: The following article describes an analysis of the spaces and the atmospheres of the protagonist's apartment in the novel Territory of Light by Japanese author Yuko Tsushima. This research concluded in the short film titled The Poetics of Home that portrays imagined, fictional spaces. The film is composed of eight chapters. Each reflecting an analytical process of reading, interpreting, imagining, tranwslating and remembering. The impalpable spaces that form in the mind during this layered play are articulated and materialized through a selection of atmospheric depictions combined into visual narratives. The Poetics of Home contributes to the study of architecture's more elusive and ephemeral aspects, those that cannot be easily researched and documented by solely utilizing classical architectural mediums, and thus suggests a method for analyzing them. At the same time, it shines a light on the often-neglected beauty of everyday ordinary spaces, that can be found in their texture, light, sound, smell, sense of time etc.

Keywords: Atmospheres; Ephemeral Aspects of Architecture; Imagined Spaces; Memories.

Corresponding author: Stefana Dilova (Alumni Berlin University of the Arts, Germany);
stefanadilova@gmail.com; http://orcid.org/0000-0002-3811-8405

»The installation was over in a couple of hours – so quickly I was taken aback. [...] every window was covered, stiflingly, in brand-new blue mesh. [...] I gazed out of a window through whose blue mesh everything appeared in a thick fog. [...] The new netting cast a bluish hue inside the apartment and made it feel smaller. An insect cage, that was it: until that moment I couldn't think what the newly circumscribed view reminded me of« (Tsushima 2019 [1993]: 65, 73).

»工事は呆気なく二時間ほどで、終わってしまった。あまりにも簡単に終わってしまった。……部屋のどの窓も、真新しい水色の縄に息苦しく覆い尽くされていた。……私は、水色の綱のおかげで、深い霧に閉ざされているように見える窓の外に眼を向けながら、答えた。……部屋の中は新しい綱のおかげで、青ずみ、狭く見えた。虫籠だ、と思った。自分の部屋の新しい眺めがなにかに似ているような気がしながら、その言葉を思いつくことができずいた«(Tsushima 1993 [1979]: 131, 147).

2.
Scenes from the Film Chapter »The Blue Mesh«, 2020–2021.

Introduction

The Poetics of Home is the outcome of an analysis based on imagined spaces and atmospheres of »home« depicted in fictional literature. In this process, spaces like this were visually rendered through the medium of film.

To implement this analysis, the novel *Territory of Light* by the Japanese author Yuko Tsushima was chosen. Eight extracts from the novel are portrayed in eight corresponding film chapters that explore the main character's apartment. Poetic descriptions of space such as light, color, shadow, material, sound, and ambience were analyzed and translated into audiovisual material; allowing for the physical perception of spaces that had previously only existed in the written word. Furthermore, the film's chapters represent fragments of my personal memories and perceptions of Japan, where I lived with my family between the ages of eight and sixteen.

The novel follows the lives of a single mother named Fujino and her daughter over the course of a year. Many of the pivotal moments take place in the apartment they share on the top floor of a dilapidated office building in Tokyo. The auto-fictional text includes various poetic depictions of the ordinary, everyday spaces of the home. The readers are invited to imagine, and phenomenologically trace, the small but somewhat cozy apartment and the way that Fujino perceives it.

The process of reading and subjective interpretation was described by the French philosopher Gaston Bachelard in his book *The Poetics of Space* (2014 [1958]: 35) as follows: »the reader who is ›reading a room‹ leaves off reading and starts to think of some place in his own past. [...] the reader has ceased to read your [the poet's] room: he sees his own again.«

During the making of this work I, its author, became the reader and interpreter of the text. In this process I would cease to »read the rooms« created by Tsushima and would start »seeing« fragments of the rooms from my own memories. The vividness of the spatial descriptions in *Territory of Light*, as well as their sincerity, captivated me and I was able to relate to them on a phenomenological level, much more than all the other texts that I had originally selected for this analysis. My relationship, and immediate attachment to the novel was surely influenced by my own lucid memories from the time I spent in Japan. Since phenomenological aspects of architecture, such as atmospheres and the perception of them, are an elusive matter that is based on subjective experience, a personal understanding of the treated subject proves to be important. It is for those reasons in particular that I decided to choose the novel by Tsushima as a basis for the development of this work. The following quote exemplifies one of the aforementioned vivid scenes that inspired this choice:

»I awoke convinced I'd overslept again, much to my despair [...]. In the dark room the TV murmured, turned down low, and from further off came a burbling of water on the boil. I remembered that I'd kept the kettle on in the kitchen since morning to warm the apartment. A cold snap had arrived with the rain the night before, but it wasn't cold enough to drop everything and get out the gas heater« (Tsushima 2019 [1993]: 75).

»音量を下げたテレビの呟き声が暗い部屋の中を流れ、遠くに、湯の滾る、軽やかな音も聞こえた。朝から、台所で湯を沸かし続け、部屋を暖めていたことを思い出した。前夜からの雨で冷え込んでいたが、あわててガス・ストーブを出すほどの寒さでもなかった« (Tsushima 1993 [1979]: 153).

While reading this passage in the novel, fragments of my own personal memories and associations layered on top of each other to create new mental images and a multi-sensory understanding of the described »dark room« (ibid.). Among other memories, I remember the sound of the TV murmuring in our neighbor's living room in Japan, the smell of the kerosene heater or even the texture of the tatami mats, along with their patina illuminated by the winter sunlight. The Poetics of Home is the outcome of the layered play between reading, interpreting, imagining, translating, remembering, and representing. The new spaces formed in the mind are articulated in the eight film chapters that render a selection of atmospheric depictions of Fujino's home into visual narratives. In order to create these narratives, the extracted poetic passages of the novel were synthesized and divided into categories such as texture, light, sound, smell, time, and season, etc.. Throughout this process I reread the novel in Japanese and in English several times. Each time I detailed the imagined spaces and dove into the distinct moods of the apartment. The most remarkable of these moods were transferred into architectural sketches, detailed cardboard models and three-dimensional animation, a film set, and a storyboard. These layers of transfer were followed by additional ones during the filming and post-production process.

3.
Scenes from the Film Chapter »Burbling of Water«, 2020–2021.

In the first film chapter, the viewer is introduced to Fujino's small apartment. A view toward the steep staircase (fig. 1) leading to the top-floor apartment is followed by fragmented views that reveal the kitchen (fig. 4), the »cubby-hole beside the entrance« that serves as a bedroom (fig. 5) (ibid.: 8), and the living room (fig. 6). An intense rain storm scene is depicted in the second film chapter »Sound of Water«. As a consequence, the building's roof overflows and water drips through its cracks. The water eventually reaches the other side of Fujino's bedroom, thus creating a »light, tenuous sound« of water »on the other side of the wall«. Although the protagonist describes a fairly commonplace problem that is rather inconvenient, her poetic descriptions of the ordeal imbue the story with a fantastical undertone (ibid.: 12, fig. 7). In the third part of the film, the summer wind is presented as an »intruder« causing the curtains in the six-mat living room to start »flapping and dancing« (ibid.: 46). This film chapter is overlaid with the penetrating sound of chirping cicadas that I remember from the summers I spent in Japan (fig. 18). The following film chapter »The Blue Mesh« depicts the spaces in the apartment with a »bluish hue« that is cast by a new netting installed on all of the windows. In the novel, the spaces are described as being reminiscent of »an insect cage«, which I imagined gave the apartment a hostile appearance (fig. 2, ibid.: 73). In the fifth film chapter »The Red Glow«, an explosion in a nearby factory is seen from the apartment and its rooftop terrace (figs. 8, 9). The reflection of the red light on different surfaces forms an extraordinary atmosphere. The sixth chapter, »The Secret Chamber« represents the room downstairs that the book's main character adores and escapes to every evening after her daughter falls asleep. She describes this room as »a room empty but for faint dancing light« as a result of the reflections caused by the neon and mercury lights outside (figs. 10, 12, ibid.: 115). The seventh chapter, »Burbling of Water« depicts a winter evening and the eighth and final chapter, »Reddish Light«, represents a sunset scene in the apartment (figs. 11, 13).

Each of the scenes are interlaced with frames from the novel's corresponding text in English which guide one through the visualized vignettes. These frames are overdubbed by my reading of the original Japanese text which is intended to strengthen the atmosphere of the scenes; making each a mosaic of translation, transformation, and interpretation.

The previously described metamorphosis of the work starting from the novel and culminating in the eight audiovisual film chapters was intended to facilitate a sensitization to everyday atmospheres that could not be easily researched and documented through the sole utilization of classical architectural mediums. Properties that play an important role in how spaces are perceived, such as the passage of time and its influence on materials, the changing seasons and the light they produce, or even the sounds in a space cannot be traced and analyzed using architectural plans, sections, one-shot renderings or models with a scale smaller than 1:1. Therefore, the sensual perception of ordinary and everyday spaces tends to be rather neglected by academic architectural research and the architectural profession. Often, the quick pace of the architectural curriculum and its deadlines, or the financial restraints of professional projects can impede the exploration of such architectural aspects. However, these aspects are fundamental to the long-lasting character of a space, how its inhabitants perceive it, and how comfortably they can live in it – the generosity it affords the lived experience.

The making of this work and its materialization of the novel's imagined spaces by conducting multiple translations enabled me to gain a very detailed understanding of the atmospheres in Fujino's home. The sounds in the kitchen, the sunlight emerging in the morning, depressive moments that hang in the still apartment air, the strangeness of the blue light that engulfs the apartment after new netting is installed on all of its windows, the sounds of the cicadas crying in the hot and humid Japanese summer nights; all of these phenomena and the feelings they conjured within the apartment became real and palpable in the course of making this work. During the filming and editing process, I even felt as if I myself would inhabit the apartment on the top floor of the dilapidated building in Tokyo. In the last days before the film was completed, I experienced a sense of nostalgia, as if I was about to move out of the apartment myself. It was a very peculiar feeling that led me to discover how far an analysis of this kind can help to expand the sensual understanding of spatial compositions.

The Poetics of Home is therefore meant to contribute to the study of architecture's more elusive and ephemeral aspects, suggesting a method for analyzing them that could ultimately allow architectural practitioners to become sensitive toward them. At the same time, it is intended to inspire a deeper observation of the everyday spaces that we inhabit, along with their hidden beauties, which could allow practitioners to see beyond the ordinary and pragmatic and therefore strengthen their design skills for the poetic space-making.

*The original Japanese text is included after each quote from the novel as it played a vital role in interpreting and imagining spaces. The English version of the novel served only as a basis for translating the project's ideas. On multiple occasions, the Japanese text enabled a more precise understanding of the poetic depictions of the spaces than the English translation.

* The figures 1–13 are stills from the film »The Poetics of Home«.
It can be watched on the following link:

stefanadilova.com/the-poetics-of-home

References

Bachelard, Gaston (2014 [1958]): *The Poetics of Space [La poétique de l'espace]*, New York: Penguin Group.

Tsushima, Yuko (1993 [1979]): *Hikari no Ryōbun (Territory of Light)*, Tokyo: Kodansha Ltd.

Tsushima, Yuko (2019 [1993]): *Territory of Light*, transl. by Geraldine Harcourt: *Territory of Light*, London: Penguin Random House.

»The kitchen and dining area immediately inside had a red floor, which made the aura all the brighter. Entering from the dimness of the stairwell, you practically had to squint« (Tsushima 2019 [1993]: 2).

4.
The Red Floor in the Kitchen, 2020–2021.

»The two-mat bedroom was as small as a linen cupboard, and I felt at home«
(Tsushima 2019 [1993]: 11).

5.
The Bedroom, 2020–2021.

»To the west, at the far end of the long, thin apartment, a big window gave on to the main road; here the late sun and the street noise poured in without mercy.« (Tsushima 2019 [1993]: 3)

6.
The Living Room, 2020–2021.

»During the night, there had been a sound of water on the other side of the wall. In my sleep I was looking out from the fourth-floor bedroom at nearby buildings bathed in rain, gleaming with neon and streetlamp colours. It was a light, tenuous sound.« (Tsushima 2019 [1993]: 12)

»(...) the sound of water in the night. That gentle, distant sound.« (Tsushima 2019 [1993]: 22)

7.
Rain Scene in the Two-mat Tatami Bedroom, 2020–2021.

8.
A Scene from the Film Chapter »An Intruder«, 2020–2021.

»My heart was racing as we went up on to the rooftop terrace together to see what had happened. (...) the beauty of the red glow that spread and intensified as I watched took my breath away.« (Tsushima 2019 [1993]: 111,112)

9.
A Scene from the Film Chapter »The Red Glow«, 2020–2021.

»Now that almost a year had passed since I took up residence, I'd actually come to feel more at home in the place downstairs than in my own apartment. (...) In the large, square, empty room (...), the darkness was tinged with the glow of the street's mercury lamps and signals and neon signs, filtering through the paper over the window« (Tsushima 2019 [1993]: 114).

10.
Scenes from the Film Chapter »The Secret Chamber«, 2020–2021.

»I went home to the apartment in the office building, which the late-afternoon sun was flooding with reddish light so bright it was almost suffocating. (...) The red floor blazed in the setting sun. It was a calm scene. Everything in it was still« (Tsushima 2019 [1993]: 122).

11.
Scenes from the Film Chapter »Red Light«, 2020–2021.

»A room empty but for faint dancing light« (Tsushima 2019 [1993]: 115).

12.
Scenes from the Film Chapter »The Secret Chamber«, 2020–2021.

»It was a calm scene. Everything in it was still« (Tsushima 2019 [1993]: 122).

13.
Scenes from the Film Chapter »Red Light«, 2020–2021.

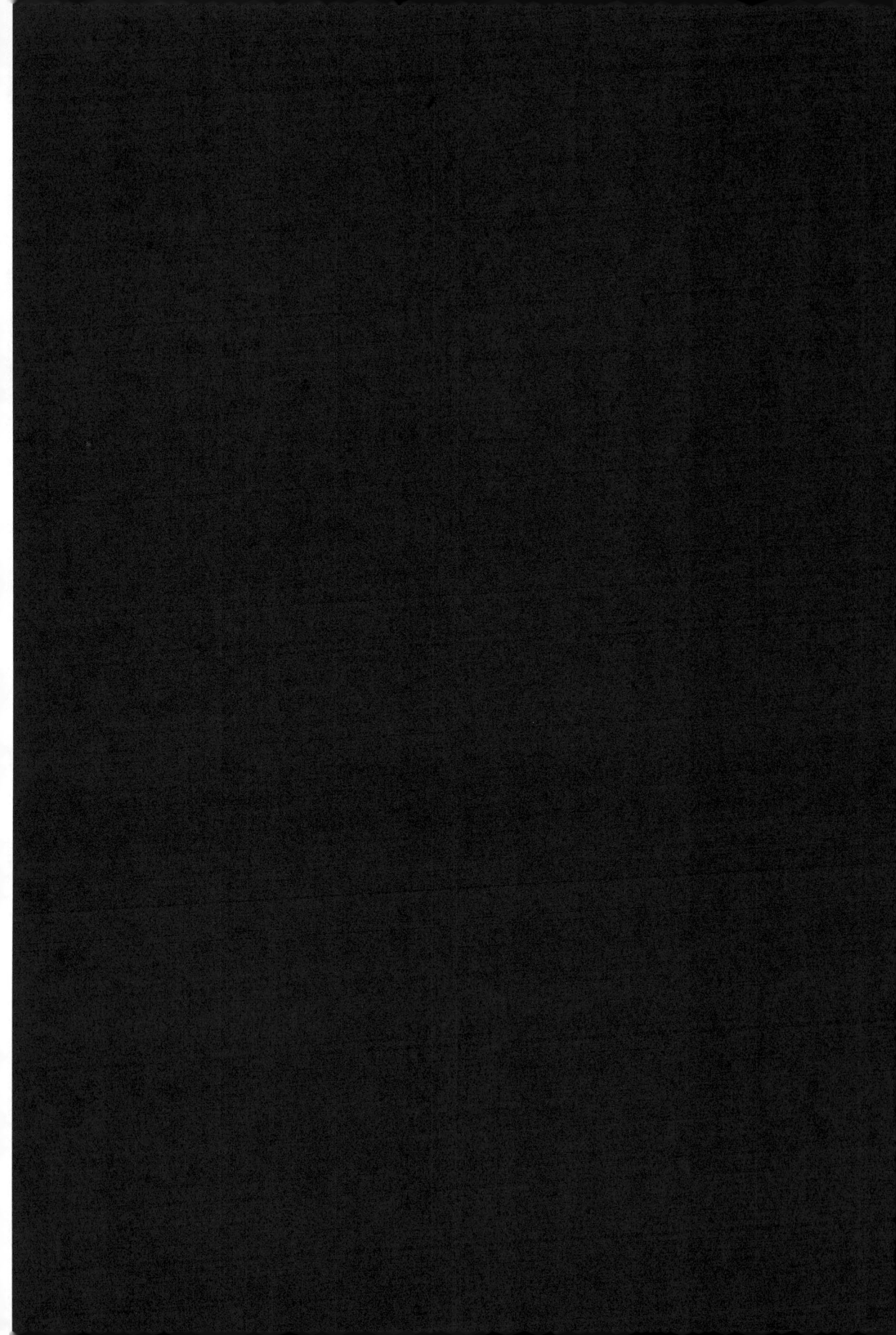

Dimensions. Journal of Architectural Knowledge, 2022-04 ∂
https://doi.org/10.14361/dak-2022-0406

Montaged Gardens – On Paper
The Red Books by Landscape Designer Humphry Repton

Achim Reese

Abstract: The Red Books represented the most important working tool of landscape architect Humphry Repton (1752–1818). To give his clients an impression of his suggestions for improvement, he used an artifice that can be understood as montage. After all, his method reveals a certain similarity to the architectural montage used by director Sergei M. Eisenstein in his essay »Piranesi, or the Fluidity of Form«. Eisenstein, however, in both his works as a director and a theoretician, aimed at overcoming a realism that had defined bourgeois art in the 19th century. Trough the work of Repton, on the other hand, the landscape garden, once an aristocratic privilege, was transformed into a bourgeois consumer good.

Keywords: 18th Century; Bourgeoisie; Humphry Repton; Landscape Garden; Montage.

Corresponding author: Achim Reese (Independent researcher, Germany);
achim.reese@gmx.de; http://orcid.org/0000-0002-4621-6291

Introduction

>In every place I was consulted I found that I was gifted with a peculiar faculty for seeing almost immediately the way in which it might be improved. I only wanted the means of making my ideas equally visible or intelligible to others. This led to my delivering reports in writing accompanied by maps and such sketches that at once shewed the present and proposed portraits of the various scenes capable of improvement« (Repton 2005: 26–27).

The fact that the landscape designer Humphry Repton (1752–1818) mentions the medium with which he tried to communicate design proposals to his clients on the first pages of his memoirs, testifies to the special importance the so-called Red Books had for his career: It was in leather-bound volumes that he conveyed plans, perspectives, and explanations to his commissioners. In many of them, he provided perspective watercolors with paper flaps. At first glance, the reader thus faced the inadequacies of the existing situation. Only when these flaps were lifted, was the »improved« state of the same site, according to Repton's plans, revealed (figs. 1–2). If one understands these flaps as montages, their functioning as a representational instrument becomes recognizable and corresponds with a certain idea of landscape design and its social and political implications. Eliding a flâneur's dérive with a daredevil attitude, traceurs (parkour practitioners) physically trace their way through the architectural landscape of the city, the suburb, or the site via dynamic movement.

Gardens for the Polite Society

In the 18th century, Great Britain was transformed from an agrarian state into an industrial and trading nation. As a result, unimaginable profits were made in the colonial economy – not least through the slave trade – and in the emerging coal and steel industries. Consequently, the new economic elite that came to lead the country was »not only made up of great landowners and members of the gentry but [...] included great financiers, city merchants and wealthy businessmen« (Williamson 2020: 42). The self-confidence of this polite society found expression in a new understanding of aesthetics and therefore, in garden design.

1.– 2.
Humphry Repton: Northrepps in Norfolk, ca. 1792,
(above) Watercolor of the condition found,
(below) Watercolor of the improved condition.
Source: Private Collection, North Wales.

The departure from the French baroque garden is then to be understood as an expression of liberal ideas: If philosophers such as John Locke deduced freedom from natural law, allegedly unadulterated nature could conversely be understood as a symbol of freedom (cf. Buttlar 1980: 9). Instead of the strict geometry of the French garden, whose beauty is particularly apparent in the plan view, the perspective of the strolling visitor gained more importance in the English garden. It is therefore hardly surprising that it was William Kent, a landscape painter, who played a significant role in the development of genuine English garden design in the 1730s. On the one hand, in his effort to create designs that resembled nature, Kent took pains to replace fences and trellises with sunken walls, so-called »ha-has«, in order to disguise the transition between the premises and the environment. On the other hand, in designing Stowe Gardens for example, he strove to express the liberal world-view of Whig Party supporters by means of a specific sculpture program and ornamental architecture (cf. Buttlar 1980: 44–53).

In contrast, not least under the influence of Edmund Burke's sensualist aesthetics, many garden designs from the second half of the 18th century aimed for a more immediate sensual effect. Thus Lancelot »Capability« Brown's designs took for their starting point the found qualities of a place (its capabilities) and aimed for their improvement. In its double meaning, the term stands for both an improvement of the agricultural infrastructure and a removal of the inadequacies of nature:

> »The eighteenth-century concept of nature in this diverges substantially from that of the twenty-first century, and at the time included existing features of landform, trees, and even avenues. These would be improved: shaped and planted not only for beauty but also to provide interest and variety« (Finch/ Woudstra 2020: 6).

Rather eschewing ornamental architecture, Brown sought to achieve diverse color and light situations, for instance, by planting trees in groups and belts, as well as by creating crescent-shaped water features known as serpentines: »It was the co-ordination of the natural and artificial elements, with as little apparent effort as possible, that perfected nature« (Finch/Woudstra 2020: 5).

3.– 4.
Humphry Repton: Betchworth in Surry, 1800,
(above) Watercolor of the condition found,
(below) Watercolor of the improved condition.
Source: Private Collection, England.

A New Business Model

In 1788, after a number of failed business ventures, Humphry Repton decided to become a garden architect and tried to establish himself as the rightful successor to Brown, who had died three years previously (cf. Rogger 2007: 11). Not only that, he, as the quotation given at the beginning of this article proves, also declared an improvement of natural conditions to be his goal. His designs with their curved hilltops, their serpentines, and the triggering of avenue plantings, especially at the beginning of his career, also reveal Brown's influence. However, Repton, who had to compete with other landscape designers in a highly competitive market (cf. Rogger 2007: 58), created an entirely new business model.

Brown, for many years the gardener of important estates, including Stowe and Hampton Court Palace, had not only contributed to as many as 250 designs but also supervised their »creation, organizing teams of laborers and employing expert contractors – earth-movers, dam builders and plantsmen – many of whom worked with him regularly over many decades« (Williamson 2020: 7 –8). In contrast, Repton had no workforce comparable to Brown's »Capability Men«. Instead, he operated primarily as a consultant: After inspecting his clients' properties, he usually limited himself to making suggestions for their improvement. He presented more than half of these approximately 400 garden designs in book form. The volumes, known as the Red Books (as they were bound in red Morocco leather) became Repton's most important working tool. This approach, however, meant that the implementation of the designs was beyond his control:

> »Some were delighted to see their places represented with anticipated effect, some insisted on my shewing more improvement than I dared to advise. Others only required the drawings to shew their friends, without ever intending to do anything to their place. [...] out of many hundred plans digested with much care, and time, and thought, few were so fully carried out in their execution, that I could be quite satisfied with my own works« (Repton 2005: 27).

However, to conclude from Repton's regret about the often inadequate implementation that he understood the books as instructions for use would be too short-sighted. Thus, a direct comparison between the recommendations outlined in the Red Books and the improvements implemented appears inadequate (cf. Rogger 2007: 12).

The fact that Repton, on the basis of specific situations, tried to make basic statements about landscape design is not least shown by his decision to subsequently publish the contents of the Red Books, thus making them known to a larger audience.

Readers were also shown the improvements proposed by Repton by means of watercolors, which were provided with paper flaps, as is common in children's books. If the viewer initially saw the original condition, the suggestions Repton had devised appeared when the flap was opened (figs. 3–4). All at once, the shorelines were found sanded, the fences removed, and the alleys broken up. New plantings hid outbuildings and lumbering opened new vistas. In other cases however, Repton, who worked first with John Nash and then with his son John Adey Repton to intertwine architecture and landscape design, also proposed comprehensive remodeling measures or the construction of new country houses (figs. 5–6).

5.– 6.
Humphry Repton: Rûg in Merionetshire, 1795,
(left): Watercolor of the condition found,
(right): Watercolor of the improved condition.
Source: Private Collection.

Montaged Landscapes

But can these flaps – if one takes Sergei Eisenstein's statements as a yard-stick – also be understood as montages? After all, the director explains in his essay »Word and Image« that the technique of montage is by no means limited to film:

> »Two film pieces of any kind, placed together, inevitably combine into a new concept, a new quality, arising out of that juxtaposition. This is not in the least a circumstance peculiar to the cinema, but is a phenomenon met with in all cases where we have to deal with juxtaposition of two facts, two phenomena, two objects« (Eisenstein 1955:14).

In his text *Architecture and Montage*, Eisenstein further states that architecture even plays a privileged role in this. While film can be understood as a path that is trodden by the eye and mind of the viewer and that, through the means of montage, can also link phenomena »far apart in time and space« (Eisenstein 1989 [1937–1940]: 116), perspective painting does not offer this possibility. Dismissing Cubism as an expression of bourgeois decadence, Eisenstein concludes that painting has never succeeded in representing a phenomenon in its multi-dimensionality: »Only the film camera has solved the problem of doing this on a flat surface, but its undoubted ancestor in this capability is –architecture« (ibid.: 117). Based on the account given by Auguste Choisy in his Histoire d'architecture, Eisenstein hence presents the visit to the Acropolis as one of the »most perfect examples of shot design, change of shot, and shot length (that is, the duration of a particular impression)«.

   If this description is applied as a standard by which to judge whether Repton's flaps can be read as montages, significant differences are to be observed: With Repton remaining committed to perspective, the path, which Eisenstein describes as a multi-dimensional experience, is realized only by the compilation of several of these perspective watercolors in a single Red Book – while the actual montage created by the use of the flaps allows only for the movement in time, but not in space. However, Manfredo Tafuri is able to discover another mode of architectural montage in Eisenstein's essay *Piranesi, or the Fluidity of Forms*. Unlike the conception described by the director in »Architecture and Montage«, this second mode does not require the viewer to put one foot in front of the other.

7.
Giovanni Battista Piranesi: Carcere oscura, 1743.
Source: Statens Museum for Kunst.

Rather, this montage is intended to set the viewer's mind alone in motion. Thus, the approach that Tafuri presents in his book *The Sphere and the Labyrinth*, not only comes closer to the cinematic experience, but also seems more apt for comparison with Repton's flaps.

In *Piranesi, or the Fluidity of Forms*, Eisenstein deals with the Carcere oscura (fig. 7), an engraving by Giovanni Battista Piranesi from 1743. Compared to the famous imaginary prisons that appeared in 1750 as Invenzione capric (fig. 8) and which were republished in 1761 under the title Carceri d'invenzione in an expanded and altered form (fig. 9), the older scene appears, as Eisenstein writes, »harmless« and »[u]necstatic« (Eisenstein 1987: 67). But it is precisely this discrepancy with the later depictions that stimulates the director's imagination: It makes him wonder »what would happen to this etching if it were brought to a state of ecstasy, if it were brought out of itself« and muses what modifications to the Carcere oscura it would take to produce the same »ecstatic effect« that is so characteristic of the imaginary prisons. He describes in detail the mental steps he takes to make the scene dissolve or even explode:

> »And now in our imagination we have before us, in place of the modest, lyrically meek engraving Carcere oscura, a whirlwind, as in a hurricane, dashing in all directions: ropes, runaway staircases, exploding arches, stone blocks breaking away from each other [...]« (Eisenstein 1987: 70).

Through these operations, Eisenstein succeeds in bringing the carefully crafted engraving of 1743 closer to the famous later etchings, characterized by a much more vivid ductus.

Tafuri states that the work of both artists, separated by many decades, testifies to the aspirations of the avant-garde: He attributes the change of Piranesi's mode of expression to the fact that the engraver no longer considered the traditional formal language appropriate for the changed reality of the mid-18th century. Likewise, Eisenstein strove to overcome a pre-revolutionary aesthetic that was perceived as ideologically questionable, criticizing that »we have received all our ›rational‹ verbal and terminological baggage from the hands of the bourgeoisie« (Eisenstein 1982: 37). By intercutting footage of the riot with a slaughterhouse scene in his film Strike (1925), Eisenstein required the viewers to bridge the discrepancy between these two images in their minds.

8.
Giovanni Battista Piranesi: The Drawbridge, 1750. First edition of the etching.
Source: Metropolitan Museum.

If the effect created by this combination exceeds the impact of the individual images, the same is true of the synopsis of Piranesi's engravings that Eisenstein, in Tafuri's view, treats like the frames of a film. And referring to Eisenstein's description of the montage as an »explosion of the shot« (Tafuri 1987: 56), he concludes that the imaginary blasting of the dungeon scene is nothing but a montage.

As he continues, Tafuri attempts to show that in the 18th century, the overcoming of an outdated formal language through the juxtaposition of divergent modes of expression also shaped landscape design. Strangely, Tafuri relates to gardens such as those designed by Brown's antipode, William Chambers:

> »In the microcosm of a ›nature educated to be natural‹, little Chinese temples, Graeco-Roman ruins, Gothic memories, magical and Arcadian settings, symbolic organisms, enchanted places add up to an evident aspiration to the synthesis of human customs.« (Tafuri 1987: 39).

In contrast to Brown's work, as well as to Repton's plans, Chambers's redesign of Kew Gardens, for example, is characterized less by an attempt to perfect nature than by the effort to assemble the most different architectural languages in one place (cf. Buttlar 1980: 74). Meanwhile, Piranesi's montage seems to more clearly find its counterpart in the flaps of the Red Books.

9.
Giovanni Battista Piranesi: The Drawbridge, 1761. Second edition of the etching.
Source: Princeton University Art Museum.

Reading between the Images

Although more than one hundred years lie between Repton's Red Books and Eisenstein's Piranesi essay, a similar concept of montage can be discovered in both cases. This montage ensures that the viewer's attention is drawn from the images themselves to the difference that opens up between the two motifs. In this way however, montage as a means of representation has inestimable value for a landscape designer who in many of his projects dispensed with spectacular interventions and instead relied on subtle measures. While design proposals aimed primarily at perfecting nature could be all too easily mistaken for actual nature, the flaps help to make the landscape designer's intervention comprehensible in the first place.

This is significant not least because Repton ascribed a sociopolitical dimension to this particular approach. After all, he regarded the English garden as a mirror of a certain social ideal – and thus as a commitment to the constitution (cf. Buttlar 1982: 143–144). In An Enquiry into the Changes in Landscape Gardening (1806), he wrote:

> »The neatness, simplicity, and elegance of English gardening have gained the approbation of modern times, as the happy medium between the wildness of nature and the stiffness of art; in the same manner as the English constitution is the happy medium between the liberty of savages and the restraint of despotic government; but while we enjoy the advantage of these middle degrees between the extremes of each, experiments in untried theoretical improvements should be made in some other country« (Repton 1806: 146).

Repton's improvements, which point to an »education« of nature as a bourgeois middle ground for the citizen between leaving nature in its wildness and subjecting it to a strict system, thus correspond to the delicate balance between the state of nature and the reign of terror. It is this idea of a subtle perfection of nature which, nevertheless, does not blur the individual features of a place, that can be expressed by the landscape designer with the help of the flaps.

* This article emerged as a first release from a research project funded by an INITIAL grant from the Akademie der Künste Berlin.

References

Buttlar, Adrian von (1982): *Der englische Landsitz 1715–1760: Symbol eines liberalen Weltentwurfs (The English Country House 1715–1760: Symbol of a Liberal World Design)*, Mittenwald: Mänder.

Buttlar, Adrian von (1980): *Der Landschaftsgarten (The Landscape Garden)*, München: Wilhelm Heyne.

Eisenstein, Sergei M. (1989 [1937–1940]): »Montage and Architecture«, transl. by Michael Glenny, in: *Assemblage 10*, 111–131.

Eisenstein, Sergei M. (1982): »Perspectives«, in: Jay Leda (ed.), *Film Essays and a Lecture*, Princeton: Princeton University Press, 34–48.

Eisenstein, Sergei M. (1987): »Piranesi, or the Fluidity of Forms«, in: Manfredo Tafuri, *The Sphere and the Labyrinth: Avant-Gardes and Architecture from Piranesi to the 1970s*, Cambridge, MA/London: The MIT Press, 65–91.

Eisenstein, Sergei M. (1955): »Word and Image«, in: Jay Leda (ed.), *The Film Sense*, London: Faber and Faber, 13–59.

Finch, Jonathan/Woudstra, Jan (eds.) (2020): *Capability Brown, Royal Gardener: The Business of Place-Making in Northern Europe*, York: White Rose University Press.

Repton, Humphry (1805): *An Enquiry into the Changes of Taste in Landscape Gardening*, London: Taylor.

Repton, Humphry (2005): *Memoirs*, Norwich: Michael Russell Publishing.

Rogger, André (2007): *Die Red Books des Landschaftskünstlers Humphry Repton (The Red Books of Landscape Artist Humphry Repton)*, Worms: Wernersche Verlagsgesellschaft.

Tafuri, Manfredo (1987): *The Sphere and the Labyrinth: Avant-Gardes and Architecture from Piranesi to the 1970s*, Cambridge, MA/London: The MIT Press.

Williamson, Tom (2020): *Humphry Repton: Landscape Design in an Age of Revolution*, London: Reaktion Books.

RECEPTION

»The gap between images that is so relevant to the idea of montage creates a tension that can be found in architecture and the arts in general.«

Ulrike Kuch: *Transmission of Knowledge, p. 38.*

1.
Lena Kirsch: »Realmontage«, (Seminar Contribution), Munich, 2020.

Dimensions. Journal of Architectural Knowledge, 2022-04 &
https://doi.org/10.14361/dak-2022-0408

Realmontage
Photographic Reading of Everyday Spaces

Max Treiber

Abstract: This contribution reflects a series of seminars that were created in a cycle of four semesters by the Chair of Architectural Design and Conception at the Department of Architecture at Technical University of Munich. Informed by the author's own research foci, a teaching concept is presented that uses photographic images to approach the perception of architectural spaces and translate them into new unfamiliar spatial models. This is a critical engagement with reality, where montage is integrated as a process-oriented and multiplying technique. The following reflection is described along with the respective exercises, a selection of works in which the students were challenged to see, explore, discover, and question the multi-layered interplay of built spaces. Under the condition of determining and acquiring analogous design methods, different topics of spatial perception and architectural design were examined. The question of how the perception of our everyday surroundings is understood as a resource of spatial phenomena and how photography can reveal new ways of seeing architecture was always at the center of the discussions. These investigations aim to expand our own repertoire of perspectives on our built environment, as well as broaden the spectrum of different design methods.

Keywords: Architectural Model; Image Repertoire; Montage; Photographic Perception; Photographic Series; Spatial Intervention.

Corresponding author: Max Treiber (Technical University of Munich, Germany);
max.treiber@tum.de; http://orcid.org/0000-0001-8117-9871

Introduction

»It has often been rightly pointed out that any art necessarily operates with montage, that is, with a process of selecting and reassembling parts and pieces« (Tarkowskij 1984: 132).

As we know, the process of montage can be formulated in different ways. Each design method has its own way of dealing with the technique of montage. However, common to all of these methods is the fact that it is a multi-layered process that occurs in several steps. In connection with a research subject, a teaching concept is presented that approaches the perception of architectural spaces with the help of photographic images and uses the technique of montage to extract spatial situations to analyze them. This established a process that highlighted new instances of existing spatial layers that revealed new conceptions of architectural knowledge.

In the first passages, a visual repertoire for the effect and experience of architectural spaces is elaborated upon, and a differentiated insight into associative techniques of architectural experience and perception outline the teaching concept. The starting point is described by the photographic image in which **Everytime Everywhere** claims that visual perception is also considered as an influential factor in everyday spaces. In **Minimal Journeys**, photographic recordings of spatial dynamics in immediate surroundings become the frame of reference for discussion in seminars. In these discussions, everyday spatial constellations are photographically examined, fragmented, and they find something **New in Known** as found material in their own spatial compositions. In this context, the photographic image is not to be understood as a representation without content but as the object of a meaningful process in design.

After outlining the individual parts of the teaching concept that build upon each other, the respective exercises **Depth advertising, Thin Veil, Frescoes en passant** and **From Image to Body** elaborate on different principles of mounting and describe the results from the production of spatial works that emerged with the discussion of everyday space. Within the four focal points, image quotations from different artistic positions refer to guest lectures (fig. 2). These images (placed in the margin), extracted from an artistic work, supported the working process of engaging with different photographic methods and anticipation with the built environment.

As it was an essential experience for participants in the seminar, this contribution also aims to stimulate the unbiased view and the **Motivation to Look Closely** at our reality, to recognize what surrounds us as thinking beings in a physical environment by quoting the Swiss sociologist Lucius Burckhardt: »to open up new perspectives, to try out ways of seeing, and to perceive the unfamiliar« (Burckhardt 2011: 108).

2.
Philipp Zwanzig: the future is now, Berlin, 2021.
(Guest lecture: February 5, 2021).

Everytime Everywhere

»Photography is in any case always surreal in its changes of scale and its constant juxtapositions, and in comprising both the conscious (?) and unconscious (?) images of a reality no longer present. Reality is being transformed into a colossal photograph, and the photomontage already exists: it's called the real world« (Ghirri 2019 [1979]: 24).

Photographs are omnipresent and the daily flood of images has become part of my everyday life. With the digital turn, the presence of the photographic has changed in a remarkable way (cf. Siegel 2014). The production and processing possibilities for photographic images are not only easily accessible to everyone but are also available everywhere and at any time in the form of the omnipresent digital camera with telephone and internet functions. This has an extreme impact on our perception – how we imagine our reality and how we view it. Everyone who does not organize their picture archive on a daily basis knows the complex moment of searching, finding, sending or showing a certain picture in a *multi-layered picture strip*. Today, I not only take pictures with the shutter release of my camera, but I also use all the download or screenshot functions of my mobile or immobile archiving devices. Then, when I am not staring at tiny screens while looking at these small pictures, I am moving between large pictures on billboards, digital screens, advertising walls and columns or masked building facades in cities (fig. 3). Photographic images move ceaselessly with me before my eyes and feet.

3.
Max Treiber: Milan, 2022.

They are wandering objects, roaming and transgressing. As the art historian Georges Didi-Huberman claims: »We cannot speak of images without thinking about their movement, their displacements and reciprocal montages in space« (Didi-Huberman 2011). The Italian artist Luigi Ghirri (1943–1992) analyzed and documented the photographic image as a phenomenon that transcends spatial boundaries in an accessible way. Trained as a cartographer, he depicted photographic and essayistic narratives of seeing. He left behind an extensive body of work in numerous photographic series where photography becomes a documentation of the duality of physical and pictorial space, and presents it for discussion about the relationship between image and space (fig. 4). With an eye for the external reality of what is mounted, Ghirri transformed the objects and situations of his everyday life into tools of conceptual reflection on space. Following his documentation, as a teacher I would like to demonstrate *photographic readings of spaces* respectively *spatial readings of photographs*, which students in seminars can use as architectural designs to sharpen their perception of built reality and use as inspiration for new ideas of space.

The aim is to trace the various potentials of the given and to investigate the horizon of meaning for one's own photographic image archive and the operation of montage with fragments of images for making space visible and conscious. Through exploring a range of possible operations of architectural montage, the results are intended to bypass the increasingly media-based and pre-defined practices of application and present their own possibilities for individual design.

4.
Luigi Ghirri: Quartiere Beaubourg, 1997, © Eredi di Luigi Ghirri.

Minimal Journeys

>The subjects are everyday objects, things found in our ordinary field of vi-
sion – images that we are used to looking at passively. Isolated from the reality which surrounds them and presented in a photograph as part of a different discourse, these images become laden with new meaning. And it's here
that we can start to look upon them actively, that we can embark on a critical
reading of them« (Ghirri 2019 [1973]: 17).

This excerpt from the text for *Cardboard Landscapes [Paesaggi di cartone]*, one
of Ghirri's first photographic series, describes essential components of the
applied method of montage in the seminars. First, there is the reference
to the everyday space in which the examination of visual perception takes
place. The familiar, the ordinary, and well-known environment were places
for empirical exploration, *minimal journeys*, as we called them in the seminar.
Explorative strolls within a small perimeter of the immediate environment
opened the students' rooms, their apartments or shared apartments in the
building block, the staircase down to the street, the neighborhood in the
district, to a wide field of numerous discoveries (fig. 5).

It was crucial that the students approached this familiar environment,
which was enriched by experiences, memories, and moods, with a neutral
view. The German sociologist Bruno Hildenbrand described this willing-
ness as taking an »abductive attitude« (cf. Steinke et al. 2003: 24-25), which
was assumed to free oneself from preconceptions in order to look at spatial
situations objectively. In this state, the discovery of spatial phenomena that
unconsciously accompanies the students' everyday life is possible. Thus, in
the first instance, the investigation pursued an open gaze on their reality.
Insofar as the exploration took place consciously, it changed the perception
of the immediate surroundings and revealed something hidden.

»This is why I'm particularly interested in the urban landscape and the out-
skirts of towns – because that's the reality that I experience every day, that I
know best and that I'm able to represent as a ›new landscape‹ subjected to an
ongoing critical analysis« (Ghirri 2019 [1973]: 17).

Following Ghirri's observation, it is important to mention that these explorative strolls were not indefinite (derivé), but that the investigations always
had an objective and a concrete field of engagement.

In the seminar, the *minimal journeys* therefore had a thematic focus and
so offered further stimuli. In addition, different perspectives on the same
topic were intended to encourage participation and discussion in the group.
Moreover, the journeys created a sensitivity to the similarities and differences caused by increasing the diversity of individual spatial effects and
perceptions (cf. Schloch 2019: 22). Thus, in the second instance, changes of
perspective on our familiar spaces, combined with a thematic orientation,
were intended to break routines and illustrate the unconscious (fig. 6).

In this step, the photographic apparatus was understood purely as a tool
of documentation. It was not taught and discussed as a machine for repro-
ducing a single moment and its technical capabilities were discussed even
less. Instead, the photographic image was conceived of as a document to be
the object of a meaningful process of recording and analyzing spaces. So it is
worth noting that when we spoke of an image here, we still meant the technical image: The image that is generated by a device (cf. Flusser 1983: 13). Like
a sketch, drawing or written note, photography allows students to examine
what they find in everyday life and add it to their repertoire. Whether they
are physically archived or immaterially stored on data storage media, these
fragments are just waiting to be inserted into new constellations.

5.
Hayahisa Tomiyasu: »Storen« (»blinds«), Zurich (2018– 2020), Film stills.
(Guest lecture: November 20, 2020).

New in Known

>>In the act of cutting out, what has been cut is set free once and for all. Freed from their contexts by the scissors, the cuttings are easier to classify, combine, and assemble in a provisional way<< (Vogel 2003: 25).

The photographic record, in which an individual piece was taken out of its context in order to acquire a new meaning in combination with other pieces, initiated the process of montage. Until this combination could take place, the various pieces were assembled, classified, and combined into a selection at the individual's will.

In spatial experiences of the everyday environment, specific domestic or urban, structural or material details were thus collected and made available in a selection for one's own work (fig. 6). Here, it was particularly important to ensure that the image detail is precisely chosen and that the viewer's focus upon the image was naturally directed to the aspects that the highlighted theme conveyed. Through a continuous connection and the displacement of various spatial images that were collected, exhibited, and juxtaposed, a treated theme became recognizable. The collection, the catalog, the series or the built-up repertoire was based on the *multiplicity*, the *diversity*, and the *hybridity* that introduced all montages (cf. Meili 2018). Thus, the photographic image collections did not serve the purpose of pure archivization. Rather, the students understood them as a starting point for the realization of a whole from various individual pieces. An unbiased attitude toward the students' surroundings, was then continued in the expanded photographic collection. The compilation, presentation, and discussion of the photographic analysis, summarized in a collection of spatial occurrences, allowed a flash of thought that led the students to further develop the topic. A recognition of something new in what already existed was assumed here as an >>abductive conclusion<< (Steinke et. al 2003: 327).

In making the collected knowledge of images and space against the background of an extracted theme explicit, the next and final step was to transform certain aspects of the accrued experience into something new (fig. 8). The results in the form of spatial artifacts, such as photographic series, performative spatial interventions or architectural models, described the familiar spaces from a different perspective on the one hand and opened up new, previously unknown spatial concepts on the other.

A variety of approaches to the photographic collection and its interpretation were revealed by this process. Different results were achieved, which in turn revealed essential components of the montage technique. Consciously and repetitively, the following insight was applied to the practice of the procedure and the description of the different results.

6.
Andreas Gherke: »Berlin«, 2020
(left): Glinkastraße (detail), Mitte, 2014,
(right): Tempelhofer Damm (detail), Tempelhof, 2016.
(Guest Lecture: June 11, 2021).

Seminar Exercises and Results

The following reflection describes four thematic focuses of spatial analysis, each of which was covered in a seminar. The seminars were always divided into at least two applied parts for architectural experience and discursive work with the photographic image. The first part usually consisted of collecting concrete spatial experiences of the everyday environment and making these explorations available by centering them in a photographic series. Through reduction, an overview and the culmination of a specific spatial theme emerged from a diverse collection. The experiences were presented in an accessible way for the group to continue thinking about them in collaborative engagement.

The second part became a continuation of the first. Building on the extracted theme, the aim was to translate the series into another analog medium. In doing so, the seminar participants left the two-dimensionality of the photographic collection and worked on the transfer into spatial depth, whether through physical models or installations.

»These photographs stand for a sense of plasticity which belongs to ordinary yet unusual views of the suburban scenario. They represent a ›state of things‹: backdrops of everyday life, waiting for something to happen, yet being already protagonists of a careful composition« (De Belle 2015).

7.
Louis De Belle: Ordinary Backdrops, 2015.
(Guest lecture: January 8, 2021).

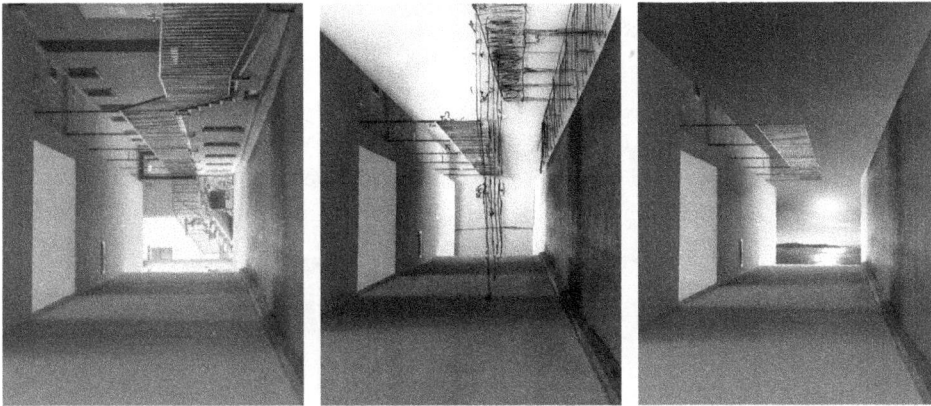

8.
Egzon Musa: »Empirical drawing journey«, From an ordinary backdrop - a courtyard passage to a house on an island. Seminar Contribution, Munich, 2020.

Minimal journeys of spatial experience and participation in lectures about different positions framed the seminar appointments (fig. 7). The joint work during the semester not only dealt with the specific photographic experience and the discussion of related topics, but also with the perception of, and influence on, architectural spaces.

The perception of one's own approach and method of working was the topic of the seminar's joint discussion and was elaborated upon in group work. The explicit thematization of the experience required a process-oriented way of working, which was continuously refined and specified in the respective process and from the insights of the seminar. In weekly meetings, participants discussed their own views using photographic series and models.

On the one hand, the participants acquired a visual repertoire of knowledge about the effect and experience of architectural spaces, as well as a distinct insight into associative techniques of architectural experience and perception (fig. 8). In addition to the production of spatial works, their experiences were recorded in self-guided accounts. Works from these are shown below and discussed within the following thematic focuses.

1. ›Depth Advertising‹*

»I put a picture up on a wall. Then I forget there is a wall. I no longer know what there is behind this wall, I no longer know this wall is a wall, I no longer know what a wall is. I no longer know that in my apartment there are walls, and if there weren't any walls, there would be no apartment« (Perec 1994 [1974]: 39).

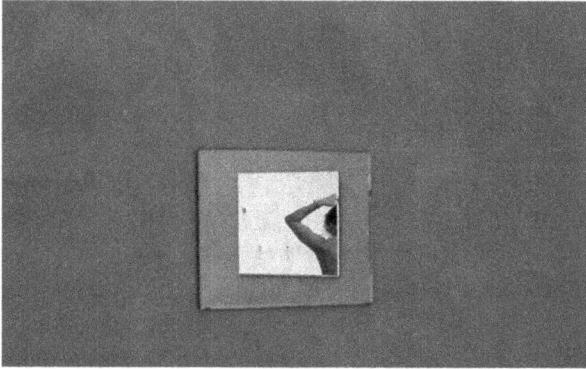

9.
Luigi Ghirri: Ile Rousse, 1976, © Eredi di Luigi Ghirri.

We began to examine the walls of our individual environment. The investigation was focused on the walls that already carry pictures within them (fig. 9). Pictures that can be found on and in walls – inside or outside – as well as pictures that are composed by walls themselves. Through explorations of the immediate neighborhood, a photographic collection that would give us a first insight into the characteristics of our walls was to be created. The subsequent process should have led to a concentration on and elaboration upon a spatial theme. With the knowledge of place, and on the basis of the extracted theme, the aim was to mount the found murals or fragments of them into real spatial situations.

At the beginning of the exercise, the focus was on the individual photographic investigation under the premise of looking closely at walls. In the process, photographic series that documented everyday walls and their fragments were created. From the walls in a room in the apartment building to the walls in the streets of the neighborhoods.

---

* The title ›Depth Advertising‹ is borrowed from a chapter in Roland Barthes' *Mythologies*

On *minimal journeys*, the personal environment was captured by ›stopping‹ and ›looking‹ in, and in front of, one's own walls. Thus, the first part of the exercise was to free oneself from any habits regarding the walls, to consider them as carriers of information and to perceive the unfamiliar: »As carriers of a considerable part of the human visual imagination« (Flusser 1993: 29).

The focus was never on the result as an absolute goal, but on the processual approach with an open result. Be it through a close look at the walls surrounding us with their materials and traces, with inscriptions and signs, with reflections of window glass or compositions of superimposed layers (fig. 10). The close observations of these projection surfaces tell stories as if by themselves. They enlighten us about the nature of tangible spatial boundaries and reveal that there is still a space behind the wall. The self-evident and banal become an adventure.

> »We began to work with a pocket mirror, creating the possibility of projecting the reflection of one window into that of the other and connecting it with the actual spatial layer behind it. [...] Through extensions and superimpositions of the views and the merging of different spatial layers, spatial montages are created that result in a change in the individual perception of space« (Georg Meck/Max Böhringer 2020: Seminar Contribution).

10.
Georg Meck and Max Böhringer: »The inner wall of the outer wall of the inner wall«, Seminar Contribution, Munich, 2020.

Here, the examination of photography left the handling of the flat image. The insights gained from the photographic collection (figs. 14–16) led to more intensive pre-occupations with spatial depth. It was no longer the image in front of and inside the wall that was the focus of observation: It was now about the space that fills the walls (fig. 17). Starting from the detached theme of the first part with rational findings, documentary photography encountered the fictional. In temporary installations, the photographically extracted theme was mounted in real space. The found spatial constellations were reshaped by interventions, which in turn produced a blurring of spatial boundaries. What began as an intimate collection became a public show. Thus, the aim was to allow the viewer to participate in the themes of reflection and mirroring, surface texture, massiveness, and fragility from the *minimal journeys* to the greatest possible adventure and thus stimulate discussion.

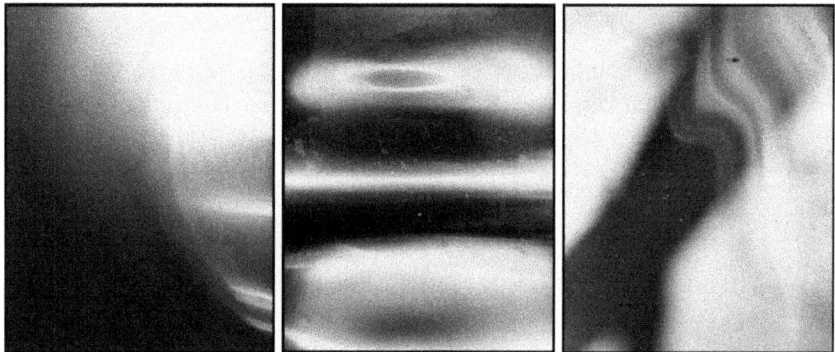

»One second. A blink of an eye. An instant. From beginning to end, the photographic project embraced the idea of the fleeting and ephemeral. [...] I understand space as a continuous and exciting moment. The reflection as a fracture of self and space. The surface as an emotional and spatial catalyst. The light as the motor of the whole. With this I recognize the motive and the aim. The material and its conditions. Its behavior, its reaction and its structure« (Juan Vintimilla 2020: Seminar Contribution).

11.–12.
Juan Sebastian Vintimilla: »Ephemeral«, Seminar Contribution, Munich, 2021.
Series (left): Aluminum photopolymer plates.
Intervention (above): »Interaction with light«.

»The wall loses its function of closed surface. Because it has been broken, has a crack or an opening, is covered by something, it becomes the ceiling or the floor. It also becomes a portal to an unknown world, a secret retreat, and a protected refuge. All this can be seen if you leave the usual scale and look very closely« (Lena Kirsch 2020: Seminar Contribution).

13.– 14.
Lena Kirsch: »The innewall of the outerwall of the innerwall«, Seminar Contribution, Munich, 2020–2021. Series (left): »Alice«. Intervention (above): Entrance Hall at Pinakothek der Moderne, Munich.

2. Thin Veil

In one of his last essays *A Light on the Wall* (1991), Luigi Ghirri describes his visit to Giorgio Morandi's studio in Bologna. In conversation with Mr. Zucchini, curator of the Morandi family archive, the latter describes a profound experience the artist underwent that created an important incentive for the following exercise:

> »right in front of his studio window, he saw an enormous 60s-style apartment block being built, complete with balconies, shutters and pastel yellow plaster. The size and colour of the building had altered the amount and quality of light entering Morandi's studio, and so he was forced to build a series of canvas structures which, when correctly positioned, could restore an acceptable level of brightness to the objects lined up against the wall of his studio, waiting to be painted. This device, which Morandi called the ›velatino‹ (thin veil) gave back to his still-life objects what the changing city had taken away, and the objects were animated by light once more« (Ghirri 2019 [1991]: 223).

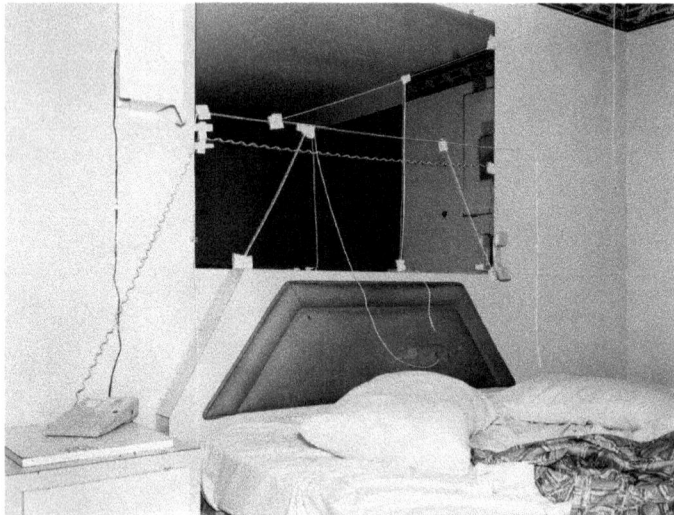

15.
Taiyo Onorato & Nico Krebs:
The Great Unreal, 2009.
(Guest lecture: 10.04.2021).

The participants climbed through the windows into their own chambers. The rooms where they spent most of their time, especially when it was largely forbidden to enter the public space (the exercise took place in hybrid form in lock-down during the Covid pandemic of early to mid-2021). In doing so, the students aimed to approach their spaces as objectively as possible.

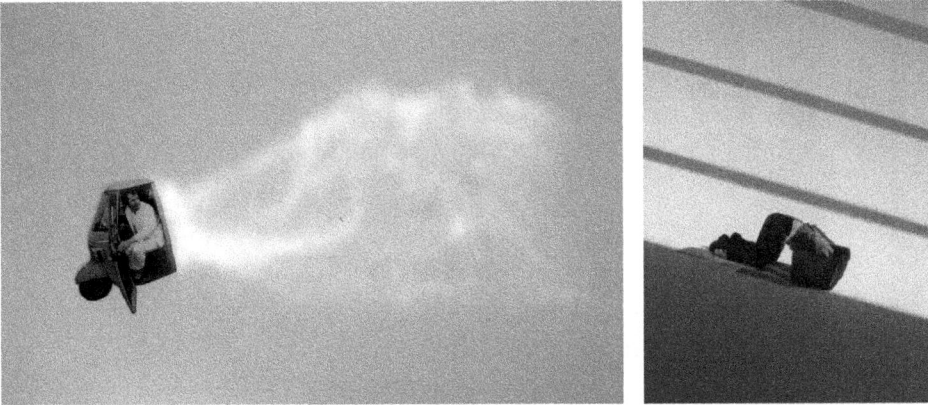

16.
Fabienne Gehrmann: »Picture fragments with light on the wall«, Seminar Conttribution, Munich, 2021.

Through objective explorations in their immediate surroundings, a photographic collection that elaborated upon a spatial theme would be created. Further along in the process, this would be which in the further transformed into a spatial installation (fig. 15). The project's focus was to become aware of the spatial dynamics and conditions within one's four walls. We had assumed that we knew our own rooms very well: The particular ›odor‹ when we opened the door, furniture, plants, and private things that give the place a personal and individual character. Different surfaces, sounds inside and outside, times of day and seasons that affect the spaces, room depths and heights, projections and setbacks, niches and hallways that make some areas busier and others less so. But how well do we really know our own spaces? In this investigation it was necessary to observe the most obvious place for a spatial engagement in order to change it.

The participants found features and situations that they didn't usually notice in their daily routine. The room of one's own became a field of experimentation (fig. 16). The means for the mounting resulted from the respective analysis. Working materials were found in the process of dealing with room inventories. Using this knowledge, the aim was to produce a room installation that referred to the extracted theme and gave the room a new sense of space.

»In the confrontation with one's own room, which one knows so well but wants to discover anew, the process of photographic collection helped to achieve a different approach to the familiar space.

Within an extensive collection of different situations in the room, the confrontation with the work of the other students was a decisive impulse in the discovery phase. Inspired by the discussion in the course, the theme of desire developed. Memories of outdoor activities and atmospheres. The need to leave the narrowness of everyday space and look upward into the wide-open space, into the inflated and slightly swaying sails, in the middle of Lake Constance, surrounded by silence, static, and yet dynamic, carried by the wind and forgotten by everything else.

The montage and installation bring this view into the narrowness of the room. The fabric divides the room by its folding and movement into areas that are nevertheless connected to each other. Suspended and stretched from the ceiling, it creates zones of space in which, despite the immediacy, I can be far away in thought and yet concentrated in the here and now« (Constantin Schindler 2021: Seminar Contribution).

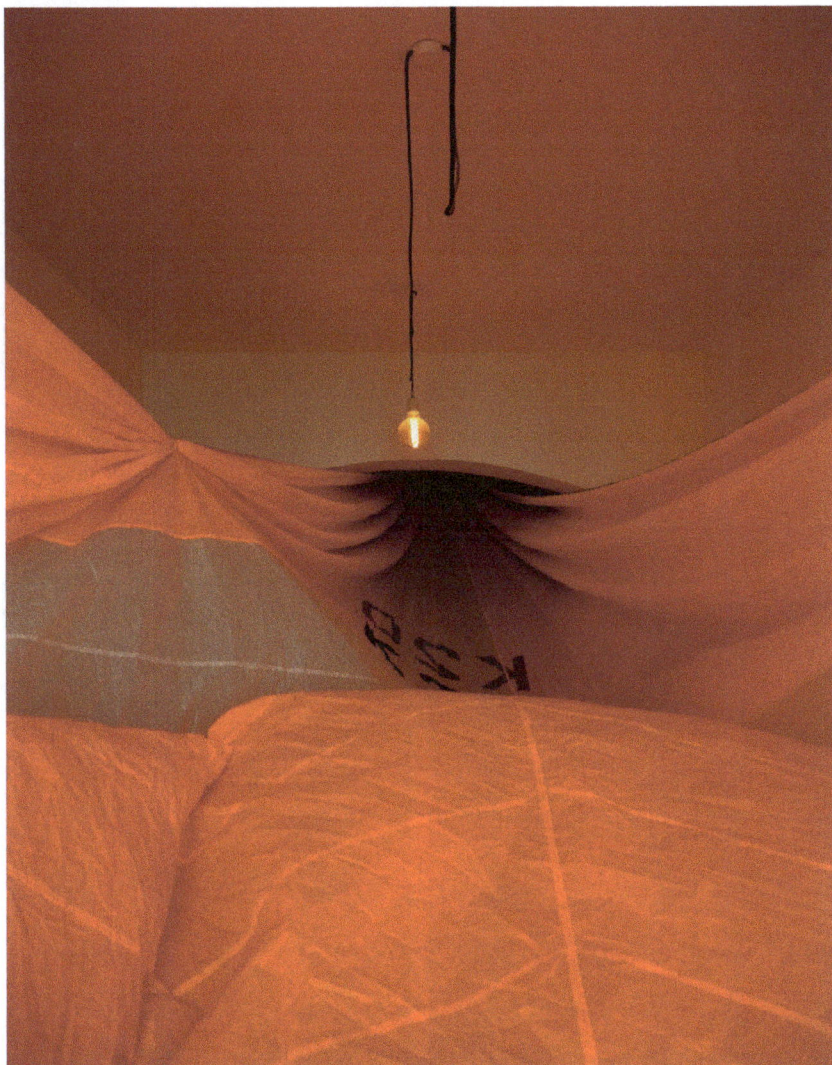

17.
Constantin Schindler: »Thin Veil«, Seminar Contribution, Munich, 2021.
Intervention (left and above).

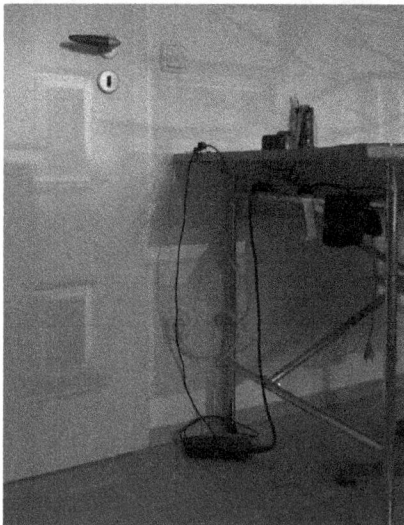

»In this series of pictures I give a personal insight into my room and my surroundings. The window becomes the projector, the walls of my room the projection surface. I use the principle of the camera obscura. I would like to invite
the viewers to look into my living space. The projection of the outside space
illuminates and sets the room in scene. Thus, each view is both a look inside
and outside. In the series, different lighting moods alternate over the course
of a day. New views of the already familiar emerge. The spatial boundaries of
my room disappear« (Tiziano Aramburo 2021: Seminar Contribution).

18.
*Tiziano Aramburo: »Thin Veil«, Seminar Contributio, Munich, 2021.
Intervention (left and above).*

3. Frescoes en passant

>The ruin opened up to me like a theatre curtain on walls that were like pages to be turned, pages full of lived experience, read as unwitting frescoes made up of signs and color, scratches, cracks and chimney smoke on chipped plaster, a real palimpsest of time« (Guerzoni 2017: 44).

19.
Franco Guerzoni: Affreschi, 1972,
Gypsum and pigment on emulsified
canvas.
Photograph: Luigi Ghirri.

20. (right)
Anna-Lena Bodendörfer: »Party
Wall«, Seminar Contribution,
Munich, 2021.

After staying at the Archivio Luigi Ghirri, I had a conversation with Franco Guerzoni in his studio in Modena in the summer of 2021. We talked about two of the series that he developed together with Ghirri. During their friendship, a collaboration developed in the late '60s and early '70s in which the two young artists explored their city, the environment, and the landscape space around Modena. In search of their identity outside the academic world, Ghirri produced a large number of photographs of the situations they found, which Guerzoni then used as a basis for adding fragments of material (fig.19). The images tell of their journeys between abandoned farms and newly completed houses; ruins and new constructions still covered with scaffolding. It indicates a discrepancy, incompleteness, and a rapidly changing world. The Affreschi and Archaeology series focus on the rawness of architectural surfaces. Like researchers in an archaeological site, they carefully and thoughtfully examined what they found.

This attempted approach to the built and changing environment became the leitmotif for the following exercise. In a thematic focus, the outer layers, the *clothes of houses* (cf. Ghirri in *Catalogo*) of the individual environment should be deciphered and translated into a spatial object within a limitation to the material of plaster. These layers span and protect the underlying body from environmental influences but even their function and appearance can be affected by various factors. Natural aging processes, sensitive areas, and exposure to stress contribute to changes. They cause cracks, wounds, and injuries to appear in the protective layer. This is followed by the process of healing, beginning with the closure of the wounds, and ending with the complete regeneration of the surface. What remains are transitions from old to new, scars, and visible color changes. These transitions form the interface with the outside world and serve as a reservoir of history and memories. Life has inscribed itself on their surface, representing the documentation and visualization of life's changing circumstances (fig. 20). Deciphering these layers could contribute to a catalog of knowledge about the life of surfaces, textures, and their appearance in reality.

»Former windows have already been bricked up, lintels exposed or plaster partially removed. An uncanny variety of compositions of colors, materials, and textures emerges. Open wounds, healing areas, bandages, and plasters. Yes, even ornaments are formed. By chance. Unplanned. A certain search for traces of the original and the new quickly emerges. Despite the raw surfaces and defensible roughness, these exposed facade surfaces had a characteristic appearance that the new was lacking« (Anna Lena Bodendörfer 2021: Seminar Contribution).

»During minimal journeys through our neighborhoods, we have noticed that the ordinary electrical box is not only inconspicuous and mostly overlooked, but has an interesting expression as a composition of basic architectural elements. Despite different manifestations and varying degrees of use, certainly the same features can always be found. A base, the foundation on which the box stands. A middle part, the facade, as protection from the outside and as a communication surface for posters, stickers and signs. And finally, the upper finish, the roof with attic. After bundling different formats and states of the electric box, it was obvious to us to translate the collage-like surfaces of the boxes into a spatial layering. With the help of acetone, the photographs could be ideally transferred to the dry plaster surface. The result was a multi-layered sculpture as an independent architectural relief« (Johann Klause, Lukas Habermeyer 2021: Seminar Contribution).

21.– 22.
Johann Klause and Lukas Habermeyer: »Electric Box«, Seminar Contribution,
Munich, 2021. Series (excerpt, left). Model (above).

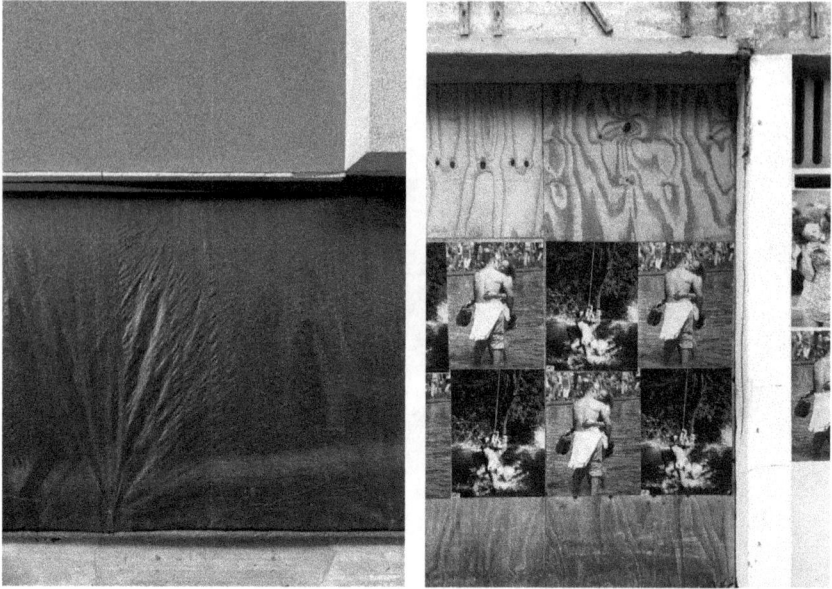

»Cutouts with frontal and clearly directed image composition. Both photographs show the encounter of facades of different textures in the surface, color, and proportion. These differences give the faces unequal weighting in visual perception. An impression that is also to be translated into a haptic effect in the context of the exercise. The skin as a sensory layer of feeling and touching, and photography as a medium of purely visual perception is to be transformed into a state that links haptic and visual perception, and largely raises the question of a haptic seeing and visual feeling« (Linus Huber 2021: Seminar Contribution).

23.–24.
Linus Huber: »Blackboard/Image«, Seminar Contribution, Munich, 2021.
Series (excerpt, left). Model (above).

4. From Image to Body

>»In these cases, considerations of gravity become as important as spatial is-
sues. The focus on material and gravity as instruments leads to forms that
were not planned from the beginning. Considerations of order are necessarily random, imprecise, and unremarkable. Arbitrary layering, loose stacking,
and hanging give the material temporary form« (Morris 2000: 108).

Released from the wall, the surface, the relief, the skin, the following
works led to an examination of spatial bodies. The observations were again
concentrated in series. An individual repertoire of spatial fragments, spatial
constellations, as well as spatial forms, emerged from the found photographic objects (fig. 25). With this collection, the aim was to assemble the
individual pieces, freed from their origin, into a coherent whole.

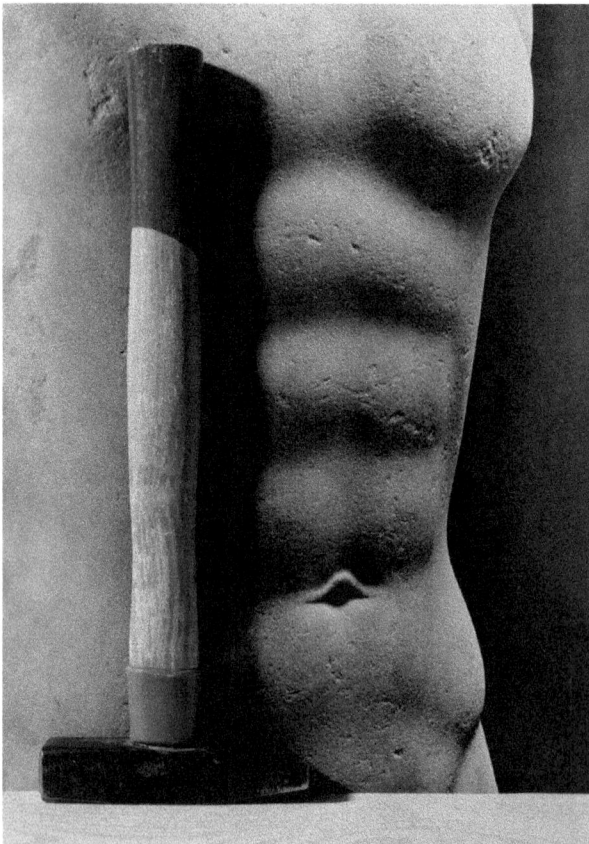

25.
*Kathrin Sonntag: »Sixpack«, (Body Parts series),
Inkjet Print, 2020.
(Guest lecture: 10.12.2021).*

The concept for the exercise was developed on the one hand from the photographic investigations of typologies as described in the works of Bernd and Hilla Becher, and the later documentaries of Lewis Baltz or Luigi Ghirri. Series of insignificant infrastructures and architectural by-products, to which we usually pay little attention, were analyzed precisely here in photographic explorations (fig. 26). On the other hand, it is true that architects also photograph, and have always photographed, as shown by the black and white images of trips taken by the Swedish architect, Sigurd Lewerentz (1885–1975)[1], who documented details, banalities, unusual perspectives, and abandoned places. In contrast, the color travel photographs of the Japanese architect, Kazuo Shinohara (1925–2006)[2], who in *Street with human shadows* exclusively portrays people in their cities surrounded by house facades. The exercise aimed to invite the viewer to engage with the ›everyday beside‹ and the resulting production of a spatial structure that brought the observations of the minimal journey to a common point.

26.
Aldis Pahl and Sven Grotheus: »statues & fountains«, Seminar Contribution, Munich, 2021.
Series (excerpt).

1   With reference to *A Trip to Italy* and *Trips around Sweden*, 2022, in: 2G Essays, Moisés Puente.

2   With reference to *Street with Human Shadows* (Kazuo Shinohara, CCA Kitakyushu, 2007) and *View from this side* (Rollo Press, May 1, 2019).

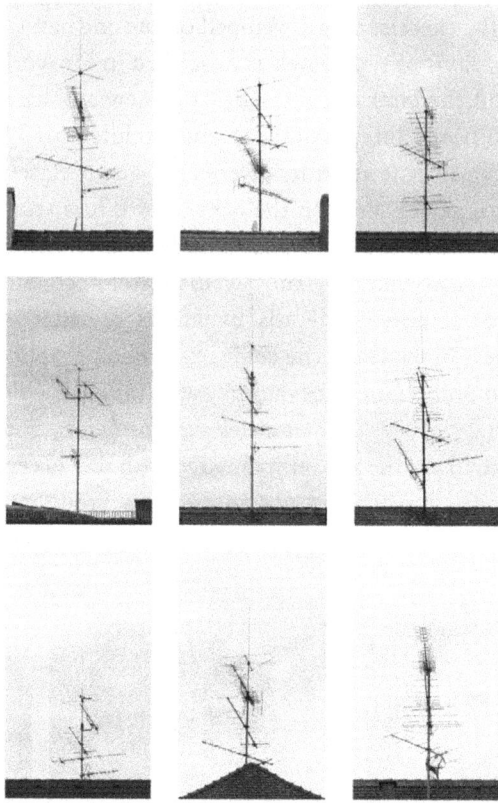

»Antennas, as everyday forms or found bodies, are concentrated into a spatial theme in a photographic series. The series illustrates the theme of the ephemeral composition of the disembodied in a field of tension between filigree and massiveness. The twelve photographs find each other for a typological image in a uniform composition. The nearly disembodied skeleton of the antennae makes use of a common vocabulary of elements that further differ in proportion, orientation, and sequence. When viewing the series, it seems as if the elements stand in a choreographic composition with each other each other, so that the structures appear seemingly from different angles as a formation of the same. The series as a starting point evokes a transformation of the disembodied skeleton into a spatial object«
»The characteristic elements of the antennae are encased in a skin of plaster and textile. They remain visible as a structural imprint and yet reveal themselves as an independent body with a fragile surface and a massive appearance«.

27.–28.
Linus Huber, Lea Maue, Myriam Wiesner: »Image/Body«, Seminar Contribution, Munich, 2021. Series (left): Munich Antennas. Model (above).

»In addition, the motif of apparent movement from the photographic series is also found in the transformation process. The now corporeal structures are brought into a common, as well as mutually movable/changeable state. In this choreographic constellation, the disembodied skeleton of the antennas becomes a spatial object whose body can be experienced as an independent space, but also together as a space between the bodies. A breeze is enough to set the bodies in motion and set the performative change in motion. With the removal of the vertical structure, the bodies become independent and yet appear light despite their massiveness. The base remains the basis as a formal analogy of the roof, but no longer of the structure, but of the frame and thus of the space in between, so that the filigree appears heavy and the massive light« (Huber/Maue/Wiesner 2021: Seminar Contribution).

»The Realmontage begins here with the close observation of a spatial object in our environment. How does the object attract our attention? What are the components of its appearance? Does it appear in different types? The photographic series provides information about this and forms the basis of formal abstraction, the decomposition of the object into its formal parameters.

In the case of the street lantern, these are four modules that determine its appearance significantly: an opaque body to hold technical components; a translucent body that protects the interior from the weather and allows the light produced to escape; four brackets that allow for easy maintenance and replacement of parts, and a contextualizing element that allows the parasitic use of the luminaire in a wide variety of environments, on pole or wire rope.

The joining principle is radically simple: folded pinning and clipping. The exploration of their aesthetic potential is the goal of a continuous design series, which continues consistently from the elaboration of the structure, through the selection of materials, to the final montage in a new object« (Sebastian Schaaf 2022: Seminar Contribution).

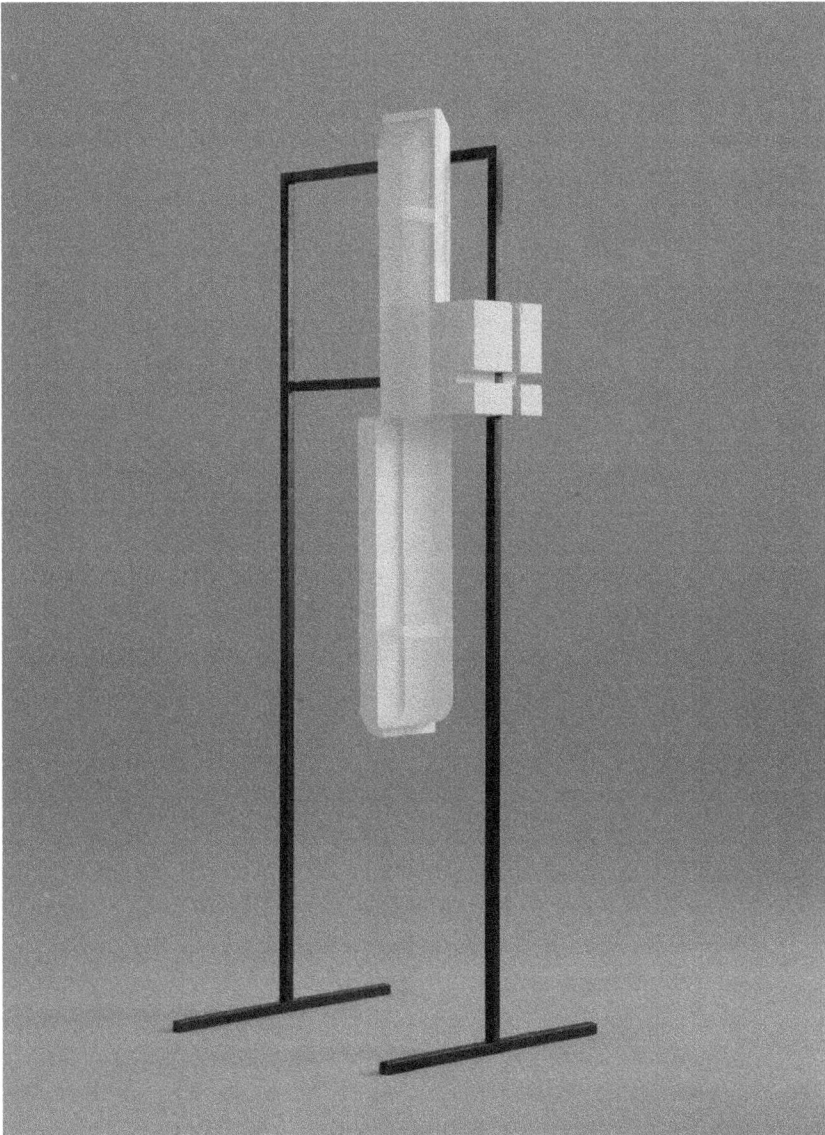

29.–30.
Sebastian Schaaf: »Object N«, Seminar Contribution, Munich, 2022.
Series (excerpt, left): Munich street lanterns. Model (above): Interpretation.

Motivation to Look Closely

>The processes we have summarized here are not an invention of our own but, on the contrary, a fairly common social practice that we intend to systematize« (Debord/Wolman 1956: 9).

Explicitly, the focused gaze through the camera lens was considered here as the starting point for a critical engagement with reality. Through repetitive/multiplying montages, new variations on an existing arrangement of spatial layers were brought to light. As such, I would like to summarize how the montages conducted here are a cohesive process on multiple levels: The process always began with the precise observation and recording of what was found and initiates the creation of a collection. In the photographic collection, juxtapositions and parallels were made visible. In addition, connections and contrasts were made on an individual level. This means memories, which photography is not capable of: A memory far from the exact precise image; a vague idea; a smell; a feeling; a stillness; a past spatial experience. These findings were in turn sharpened into a spatial theme and found a new expression in translation. With this transformation into an artifact in its own right, there was a modification of what was found, as well as a reconnection to its origin. The physical presence of the new, for which no concept yet exists, showed the sum of the collected qualities: A forged relationship between existing, prefabricated entities that provoked the emergence of unexpected, new qualities.

The motivation for this research and teaching is that the perception of our everyday spaces, as well as the effects of image production overall, are increasingly becoming the subject of architectural debates. Thus, the process that has been systematically addressed here is one of many ways with which to engage more intensively with the spaces we find every day, on the one hand, to gain insight into their essential characteristics and dynamics and on the other hand, to sharpen the ability to trace a physical connection between oneself and the surrounding reality.

A final note of thanks goes to all the students for their inspiring outputs that enrich this issue and to the guests for the stimulating inputs, as well as to the openness of the chair, which made the free-working method possible and supported it.

References

Barthes, Roland (1964 [1957]): *Mythen des Alltags [Mythologies]*, transl. by Helmut Scheffel, Frankfurt a. M.: Suhrkamp. – English translation: *Mythologies*, transl. by Annette Lavers, New York: Hill and Wang, 1972.

Burckhardt, Lucius (2011): *Spaziergangswissenschaft, Warum ist Landschaft schön?*, Berlin: Martin Schmitz Verlag. – English translation: *Why Is Landscape Beautiful?: The Science of Strollology*, edited by Markus Ritter/Martin Schmitz, Basel: Birkhäuser, 2015.

De Belle, Louis (2015): »personal website«, https://www.louisdebelle.com/ordinary-backdrops/, accessed October 30, 2022.

Debord, Guy-Ernest/Wolman, Gil J. (1956): »Mode d'emploi du détournement«, in: *Les lèvres nues n°8*, Bruxelles. – English translation by Ken Knabb: »Methods of Detournement«, in: Ken Knabb (ed.): *Situationist International Anthology*, Berkeley, CA: Bureau of Public Secrets, 8–14, 1981.

Didi-Huberman, Georges (2011): *Experimenter pour voir / Experimentieren, um zu sehen (Experimenting to see)*, http://www.dgae.de/wp-content/uploads/2011/09/Didi-Huberman.pdf, accessed November 15, 2022.

Flusser, Vilem (1993): *Dinge und Undinge: Phänomenologische Skizzen (Things and Non-Things: Phenomenological Sketches)*, München: Carl Hanser.

Flusser, Vilem (1983): *Für eine Philosophie der Fotografie*«, Göttingen: Vice Versa Distribution, – English translation: »Towards a philosophy of photography«, Göttingen: Vice Versa Distribution, 1984.

Ghirri, Luigi (2019 [1991]): »A light on the Wall« [Una luce sul muro], in: Luigi Ghirri, *The Complete Essays 1973–1991*, London: Mack, 223–226. – Originally published in Italian: Ibid.

Ghirri, Luigi (2019 [1979]): »Kodachrome«, in: Luigi Ghirri, *The Complete Essays 1973–1991*, London: Mack, 23–26. – Originally published in Italian: Luigi Ghirri, *Niente di antico sotto il sole: scritti e limmagini per un'autobiografia*, Torino: SEI, 1997.

Ghirri, Luigi (2019 [1973]): »f/11, 1/125, Natural Light« [Diaframma 11, 1/125, luce naturale], in: Luigi Ghirri, *The Complete Essays 1973–1991*, London: Mack, 35–38. – Originally published in Italian: Ibid.

Guerzoni, Franco (2017): *Ouvre*, Milan: Skira, 2017.

Meili, Marcel (2018): *Unicum*, Berlin: Ausstellungskatalog der Architekturgalerie.

Morris, Robert (2000): »Anti Form«, in: Robert Morris, *Continious Project Altered Daily: The Writings of Robert Morris*, Cambridge/MA: MIT Press, 255–258.

Perec, Georges (1994 [1974]): *Species of Spaces and Other Pieces [Espèces d'Espaces]*, Munich: Peinguin Random House.

Schloch, Aline (2019): »Die Spaziergangswissenschaft/Perlentauchen in der Stadt« (»The Strollology/Pearl Diving in the City«), in: Christophe Girot (ed.), *Auf Abwegen, Pamphlet 23*, Zürich: gta Verlag, 11–20.

Siegel, Steffen (2014): *Belichtungen. Zur fotografischen Gegenwart*, München: Wilhelm Fink.

Steinke, Ines/Flick, Uwe/von Kardorff, Ernst (eds.) (2003): *Qualitative Forschung. Ein Handbuch (Qualitative Research: A Manual)*, Hamburg: Rowohlt.

Tarkowskij, Andrej (1984): »Über Zeit, Rhythmus und Montage« (»About Time, Rhythm and Montage«), 131–141, in: Andrej Tarkowskij, *Die versiegelte Zeit (The sealed time)*, transl. by Hans-Joachim Schlegel, Berlin/Frankfurt a. M.: Ullstein

Vogel, Juliane (2003): »Mord und Montage« (»Murder and Montage«), in: Bernhard Fetz/Klaus Kastberger (eds.), *Die Teile und das Ganze: Bausteine der literarischen Moderne in Österreich (The Parts and the Whole: Building Blocks of Literary Modernism in Austria)*, Wien: Verlag Paul Zsolnay, Profile 10, 22–43.

1.
Burkard Meyer Architects: »BBB Martinsberg«, Baden, Switzerland.
Photographs, 2006.

Dimensions. Journal of Architectural Knowledge, 2022-04 ᵊ
https://doi.org/10.14361/dak-2022-0409

Montage
From Images to Narratives

Erieta Attali

Abstract: The introduction of the montage technique into my photography through the application of narrative sequences allowed me not just to revisit, but also to creatively re-interpret
and use work that spans my 30-year photographic practice, and combines archival material with
new photographs and geographically discontinuous locations. A narrative sequence allow a series
of photographs to unfold and to communicate the sense of approaching a work of architecture
from multiple standpoints within the landscape. This is achieved either through the juxtaposition
of multiple images in the same space or surface, but also within a single image whose two-dimensional space collapses a multiplicity of standpoints by layering transparent and reflective
surfaces that are found on the photographic subject itself. These external (multiple images)
and internal (multiple reflective and transparent surfaces within one image) juxtapositions also
expand the reach of the image into a wider range of temporal scales: from the instant shift to
the daily, the seasonal, and the historical. My use of montage narrative sequences started with a
desire to codify and communicate the act of the »architectural walk« which for me is an essential process of engagement with the photographic subject and its context that usually lasts for
several days. Gradually, it expanded into a general visual language that attempts to articulate the
spatial and temporal interplay between architecture and landscape.

Keywords: Double Exposure; Layering; Motion; Narrative; Sequence; Temporal Scale; Time.

Corresponding author: Erieta Attali (National University of Singapore, Republic of Singapore);
erietaattali@gmail.com; http://orcid.org/0000-0001-5986-1161

From Images to Narratives

Since my earliest early days as a photographer I was employing narrative elements in my work, but not in an intentional, or structured way at first. These elements, represent an attempt to create particular moods or elicit emotional responses by treating inorganic matter as filmic characters performing within the landscape. The characters might be inanimate but they take many forms: from mineral formations, ruins, and human traces on the ground to hardy outcrops of vegetation, contextualized in a way that emphasizes their presence in, and habitation of, the landscape. They are cues, which, when embedded within single images have the power to conjure an (often implicit) storytelling framework. I did eventually discover, however, that the narrative power of photography really unfolds when explored through a series of photographs viewed in curated succession.

The recent introduction of the montage technique into my photography encouraged me to revisit and to creatively re-interpret and use work that spans my entire career, thus combining archival material with new images. While photographers like Hungarian-British photographer Mari Mahr focused on the personal domain and used photography as a tool to construct memories by reframing objects that she inherited and cherished, in my recent work, the memory-making is at the scale of the place and the landscape. Montage has allowed me to expand photography into a visual language for reading spatial and temporal relationships between culturally, geographically, and even semantically, disparate places and conjure new, hybrid realities.

2.
Top: Studio Granda: Hof House, North Iceland, Iceland,
bottom: Atacama Desert, Chile, both 2015.

3.
Dan Graham: »Heart Pavilion«, Philadelphia, USA.
Photographs, 2001.

The Montage Process: Building Narratives through Multiple Images

Much later in his career, British painter and photographer David Hockney started employing a similar technique, namely collage, in order to add depth and three dimensionality to his cityscapes. Similarly, my intention when juxtaposing photographs is to communicate the sense of approaching a work of architecture from multiple standpoints within the landscape. Of course, the static image cannot – and should not – compete with filmography in communicating a smooth and continuous movement through space. It can however – as the cubist painters discovered more than a century ago – be employed as a different kind of storytelling tool, where fragmented moments aggregate, and spatial and temporal layers collapse into each other and reveal unseen relations. In that respect, the static, two-dimensional condition of photography enhances the narrative element and invites the viewer to actively engage with the layers, and re-build a story themselves. So far, I have employed glass and successive layers of reflections in order to capture this multiplicity of standpoints; now, I investigate it by employing transparent natural elements, such as fog or masses of see-through foliage, but also by juxtaposing several photographs. The collapsed layers and longer exposures do not only capture spatial complexities, but also temporal continuities and transitions. These transitions cover a large spectrum of time scales which require different synergies of material and light, from the instant shift to the daily, the seasonal, and the historical; the latter of which eventually causes the absorption of everything by, and the transformation of everything into, landscape. When trying to capture a rate of change that feels close to our daily experience of our environment; air, water, and vegetation are essential components, since they are sensitive and pliable enough to capture rapid transitions. These transitions are vital in communicating the experience of existing in a place, occupying it, and merging with the context, but also in creating what we commonly describe as atmosphere or mood: the intangible, ephemeral, emotional content of a scene. While air is invisible, its effect on receptive materials in the environment can be captured through long photographic exposures. The aural component of the wind, which is central to its perception, cannot be carried through by image alone, but the ghostly traces implying the movement of water or foliage is usually enough to evoke it in an almost synesthetic way.

Pathfinding as a Story Drive

As a photographer I do not build installations, but the path is an element of the landscape that also features heavily in land art constructions. Paths allow me to communicate both the physicality of the process of photographing outdoors and the sequential nature of the itineraries that I need to follow on foot, often for tens of miles and while carrying heavy photographic equipment.

The path narrates possible pasts and futures: it could be the way that the spectator accessed the landscape or the way out of it. For me, it often signifies the next destination, the next turn in a journey to reach the ever-shifting edges of personal geographies. Pathway-like objects are also a very distinctive marker of time, describing in a very clear, albeit nonverbal way, the pattern of use of a given space and the accumulated temporal trace of that use. In nature, the path is – usually but not always – the erosive result of human presence: it turns us into yet another entropic natural process, therefore connecting us with the landscape on a deeper level. In architecture, when consciously designed, the path is a fundamental building component of the narrative of using space. Engaging with these architectural paths allows me to approach the continuous spatial experience of living with and within architecture, instead of producing a static, mute image. If one thinks of the montage process as the application of a visual grammar in order to compose narratives, then paths work as verbs. They connect the other elements; the nouns or characters of the visual narratives through action and motion.

4.

Paths, Singapore, 2021.

5.

Marc Mimram: TGV Train Station, Montpellier, France, 2017.
Double Exposure Photograph, 2018.

6.
Top Left: Angelo Bucci, sbpr Architects, House in Sao Paolo, Brazil, Photograph, 2009.
Top Right: RCR Architects, Pedra Tosca Park, Olot, Spain, 2004. Photograph, 2013.
Bottom Left: Olavi Koponen, Doctor House, Island of Halskar, Finland, Photograph, 2009.
Bottom Right: Bernard Tschumi Architects, Lerner Hall, New York, Photograph, 2000.

7.
Kengo Kuma Architects & Associates: Glass Wood House, New Canaan, USA.
Photographs, 2015.

Movement in Nature and Architecture: Case Studies

I have been aware of montage and image sequences as photographic tools, but did not attempt to use them for several years. My focus on liminal landscapes purged of human presence did not seem like a fertile ground for such a mode of expression. Through my ongoing research however, I came to reconsider the various elements of the narrative toolbox as I slowly realized that my own approach already heavily employed temporal themes.

The Glass Wood House photographic case study in New Canaan (Kengo Kuma & Associates) allowed me to fully embrace the sequence not only as a way to express temporality in different scales, but also to communicate continuity in the experience of space and connect my early work to my current photographic research.

By focusing on a localized geography marked by seasonal transformation, it became possible to identify varying scales, rates, and intensities of interchange between a built object and its context. This series would open up a new world of possibilities for me through the use of narratives and the discovery of notions of transparency in natural materials. My use of montages-narrative sequences started with my desire to codify and communicate the act of the »architectural walk« which for me is an essential process of engagement with the photographic subject and its context that usually lasts for several days. Conversely, my very long – almost two- year – involvement with the Glass Wood House also helped me to refine the concept of transparency in nature. As the seasonal cycles encased the glass house in layers of snow, auburn leaves, green grass, and floating petals, the relationship between the man-made transparent glass and the natural diaphanous layers of vegetation became increasingly ambiguous. Walking around the photographic site is as important in my work as taking the final picture. I need to experience the site throughout the day. I pay repeated visits and take notes, and exploratory shots, with the aim of grasping the transformational process that both the building and landscape experience: the pulsations of natural light, the dispersing of shadows, the degrees to which the building blends, or stands out. Every photograph is a result of this engagement with the spirit of the place and a distilled experience that stems from a kinematic, dynamic experience.

Therefore, in trying to evolve my work and expand my means of expression I want to show this peripatetic process. Structures and natural formations unfold gradually as one moves around the interlocking masses. Shapes materialize through transparent layers of vegetation, glass or vapor only to disappear again within a few steps. These thresholds of transition are vital in understanding the interplay between architecture and its context, and it is precisely those thresholds that I wish to explore through the sequence. Instead of simply sharing the final image, or even final few images, I want to invite the viewer to explore the site with me and build an understanding of the place that it would not be possible to achieve, under normal circumstances, via a static printed image.

Of course it is not only the photographer that moves throughout the site: the natural environment is an orchestra of elements in motion. Photographic montages and sequences allow me to further clarify the investigation that I have so far conducted with single images, which focused on the precise threshold of transition. From the wind that animates vegetation, to the rapidly dwindling late-afternoon sunlight and accumulation of volatile storm clouds, photographic sequences facilitate the folding of a living three-dimensional space into the two-dimensional surface of a photograph.

8.
Oceanscape, Tasmania, Australia. Photographs, 2016.

9.
Oceanscape, New South Wales, Australia. Photographs, 2016.

When I set out in 2013 to photograph the work of RCR Architects in Olot, a glass pavilion hotel with a limited number of rooms all made out of glass, it was not my initial intention to try and create a temporal series, spanning the whole day. The overlapping layers of glass reverberated like kaleidoscopic spaces during the day, blurring the spatial distinction between rooms, corridors, common spaces, and the outside. The same floating membranes of glass turned into a claustrophobic mirrored cage during the night, where all my external references were absorbed and then vanished. In many ways, I was already composing montages in Olot, only the multiplicity of images was hiding within a single picture; embedded in the space thanks to the material properties of glass.

This realization eventually led me to re-examine the work of photographers who tried to express themselves through temporal, but also montage series that unfold as narratives. In retrospect, Olot was one in a series of experiences that forced me to consider my responsibility as a photographer of space, eventually rejecting the reductionist approach that tries to distill a couple of static images out of something so pliable and fleeting.

For this reason, I have been trying to formulate, and understand, all the narrative methods that I gradually accumulated through my work; sometimes instinctively and sometimes intentionally. I have used internal montages where reflective and semi-transparent surfaces create spatial multiplicities in a single image. The internal montages are complemented by internal narratives, inanimate characters, paths or traces of motion captured in long exposures that implicitly position the image within a larger story that is ongoing or undecided. Then there are the external montages, meaning a literal juxtaposition of several images that are linked into an episodic narrative. Internal and external cues and sequences link up together, and articulate subjective, hybrid realities which form the scaffolding for narratives. These narratives are instrumental in placing the viewer within the world that I am trying to create, and in the end, represent for me attempt to connect with the transient nature of architecture and the landscape that it is inevitably part of.

10.
RCR Architects: Les Cols, Glass Pavilion, Spain. Photographs, 2014.

11.
RCR Architects: Glass Pavilion, Les Cols, Spain. Photographs, 2014.

Dimensions. Journal of Architectural Knowledge, 2022-04 ᴥ
https://doi.org/10.14361/dak-2022-0410

Artistic Practice as Preservation Process
The Performative Potential of Montage

Katrine Majlund Jensen

Abstract: With its creation of fissures and fragments, the montage is uniquely positioned to question the representational power of architecture. When related to the field of preservation such a gesture conflicts with preservation's traditional urge to reinstall and complete the architectural fragment into a grander narrative and its underlying leitmotif of authenticity and integrity. From an analysis of Alex Lehnerer's and Savvas Ciriacidis's installation *Bungalow Germania*, the paper explores the possibility of an experimental and critical notion of preservation. A notion emerging from the artistic strategy of montage which frames the fragment as productive rather than reductive. With that, preservation might become a creative just as much as restorative field of practice.

Keywords: Architectural Heritage; Experimental Preservation; Fragment; Performativity; Montage.

Corresponding author: Katrine Majlund Jensen (Brandenburg University of Technology, Cottbus, Germany);
Katrine.Jensen@b-tu.de; http://orcid.org/0000-0003-4353-3491

Introduction

Experimentation and preservation are rarely seen as two sides of the same coin. Rather, the preservationist is commonly seen as the expert that practices the care and maintenance needed to keep the historical object as heritage. This article advocates for an expanded notion of preservation however: a notion where privileged access to the historical building holds the promise of a creative rather than restorative field of practice. As creative practice, montage is experimental in nature. Through rupture and juxtaposition, it provokes the convenience of reading signs as fixed representations.

Based upon an analysis of Alex Lehnerer's and Savvas Ciriacidis's spatial montage *Bungalow Germania*, this article suggests that the installation is an experimental preservationist intervention.

It aims to explore preservation as a practice which moves architectural heritage from a representational to a performative mode of being. The outcome might be heritage as a process of negotiation rather than as an object of visitation. This article contains an outline of the discourse of experimental preservation and the artistic strategy of montage, followed by an analysis of *Bungalow Germania* and how it places representational architecture in a performative mode of being. Finally, this will be considered as an experimental preservationist practice.

Experimental Preservation

To be experimental in the preservation of architectural heritage has rarely been seen as an asset. Here, experimentation appears as a threat, which itself provides a clue about how the role of preservation has been perceived. Nonetheless, experimentation is proposed as a game-changing approach in the book *Experimental Preservation* (Otero-Pailos et al. 2016). With contributions from Jorge Otero-Pailos, Erik Fenstad Langdalen, and Thordis Arrhenius among others, it is ostensibly a conversational book that provides a manifesto-like discussion between case studies and has the aim of exploring preservation as a self-reflexive practice. »The starting point is doubt« as Otero-Pailos states, and with that the book positions itself as a critical alternative to what it defines as »the longstanding identity of preservation with the governmental protection of cultural objects, and the largely unquestioned narrative that preservation bureaucracies always act for the common good« (Otero-Pailos et al. 2016: 11, 20).

What was a threat is now turned into an operational doubt. When occupying the experimental as a position that conceptually and practically tests what is relevant knowledge within architectural preservation, the possibility for widening the definition of what it means to preserve has been given. Experimental preservation is therefore interdisciplinary preservation too, the preservationist being both inside and outside this field. To provide a lens where the strategy of montage can be perceived as an experimental preservationist action, a reinterpretation of two fundamental elements of preservation is useful: how it defines its object and its tool of intervention.

Object

A common understanding might be that preservationists work on objects that are already intrinsically defined as heritage. This has long positioned the preservationist as a technical doer who possesses the expert knowledge necessary to practice the care and respect required by the architectural heritage object. Whereas the experimental preservationist might choose objects that are already canonical or enrolled in what Laurajane Smith has termed the »Authorized Heritage Discourse« – referring to the governmental and official choices of heritage that current generations »must« care for – the experimental approach to such sites would attempt to make the preservationist's work visible as being discursive (Smith 2006). The aim is to discover new latencies and to show that preservation in its protective sense is never a neutral practice but a strategic amplification of the object as canonical. Unlike many modernist architects that also had the experiment to an end itself, the experimental preservationist uses experimental, artistic, and creative strategies with the aim of testing their object's potential for heritage (Otero-Pailos et al. 2016: 11–20). The act of testing, rather than stabilizing the cultural object, becomes here, the preservation work itself. Consequently, preservation becomes a way of overtly co-creating the heritage object or querying its potential as such.

Intervention

Intervention has always been a key element in the preservationist's toolbox and much preservation theory has consequently revolved around the degree to which intervention into historical architecture is appropriate, and how. Likewise, intervention is a key component for the experimental preservationist. While intervention is traditionally associated with care and maintenance – even if a philosophy of minimal intervention – an experimental approach needs intervention to actively question our relationship to a given object. Whereas intervention, in a more conventional understanding, has had an affirmative aim in seeking to uphold a certain meaning reserved for an object, the experimental approach intervenes to test the interpretive boundaries for an object, sometimes to the extent of the collapse of meaning (Otero-Pailos et al. 2016: 20). Within this understanding, preservation becomes a practice that uses intervention to explore the illusory aspects of heritage and question it as a self-explanatory given. Intervention is thereby connected to how experimental preservation is a practice-based critique of the privileging of the »old, grand, prestigious, expert-approved sites« within preservation, using the realm of sensuous experience as a method of questioning architecture as testimony (Association of Critical Heritage Studies n.d.). Consequently, the experimental paradigm uses intervention not from an objective of care and maintenance but to play with boundaries, modification, re-contextualization, and contrasting. It is in this way that the architectural montage is not only an artistic practice but can be seen as part of an interventionist toolbox of experimental preservation.

The Artistic Strategy of Montage

Well known from avant-garde and modernist art, montage refers to how different elements are joined together or juxtaposed to form a new whole and meaning. As an artistic strategy, it frames the signifier as discursive and dialectical: »The dialectical mission is to fuse fragments as concentrated form; the discursive one is to create fissures or interruptions in the established order« (Druckrey 1994: 5). Connected to the experience of modern urbanity, montage has been used as both experimental artistic expression (from Dada to constructivist art), as cultural comment and critique (as in the example of Walter Benjamin's *The Arcades Project* using montage as an approach to a new historiography (Benjamin 2002), as well as an architectural principle the 1920s Russian film-maker and propagator of the montage,

Sergei Eisenstein, indeed saw montage as an essentially spatial term, with the architectural path as significant, where »the spectator moved through a series of carefully disposed phenomena« (Eisenstein 1989 [1937–1940]: 119). As Michael Newman writes, montage »allows for the constitution of subject positions which are dynamically entered into, or even repudiated by the viewer/reader/interpreter, who participates with the ›author‹ in the creation of the work« (Newman 1989: 45). Unlike collage, the technique of montage places greater emphasis on juxtaposition, often with the aim of making a rhetorical point. Furthermore, this links to the political roots of montage as an art form used for its subversive potential, which resulted in the art form waning in 1930s Germany and the Soviet Union, owing to these societies' increasing suppression of experimental aesthetics. In this line, Joshua Sperling however, argues how nowadays, montage has been freed from its political and historical roots and most commonly refers to an associative rather than a narrative logic (Sperling et al. 2016: 294). While the creation of an associative rather than a narrative space might also account for the montage of *Bungalow Germania*, the installation arguably points at the relevance of montage within architectural discourse to question established orders and authority beyond mere aesthetic principle.

1.

Alex Lehnerer and Savvas Ciriacidis: Bungalow Germania, Venice, Italy, 2014.
»Helmut Kohl's car staged in front of the facade of the German pavilion«.
Photograph: Bas Princen.

Bungalow Germania

As the German contribution to the Venice Biennale of Architecture in 2014, *Bungalow Germania* was created by architects Alex Lehnerer and Savvas Ciriacidis. It brought together two buildings with overtly political pasts: One was the German pavilion in the Giardini della Biennale in Venice itself, the other a partial replica of the chancellor's bungalow (*Kanzlerbungalow*) in Bonn, cross-cutting the German pavilion and creating a montage of two architectural languages and histories (Lehnerer/Ciriacidis 2014).

Originally constructed as the Bavarian pavilion in 1909 by Daniele Donghi, the German pavilion claimed its current name in 1912. However, its architectural styles and meanings have changed throughout history and it was fundamentally remodeled in 1938 by the architect Ernst Haiger, whose design language was that of the neoclassicism commonly used in Nazi Germany (Heilmeyer 2014). With its massive pillars, symmetry, and clearly defined entrance it was in line with National Socialist aesthetics and formulated a statement of power in stone, communicating a message of subordination to its visitor. In 1964 the pavilion went through its last significant renovation, in which a wall and dropped ceilings were removed in order to make a central space with more light (Lehnerer/Ciriacidis 2014).

Its political history has recurrently sparked controversy about the pavilion's future fate; with some curators and public voices advocating for demolition (Oelze 2011; Paterson 2010). Exhibits in the pavilion have therefore increasingly shown an awareness of the space as a historical political setting and not just as a backdrop for exhibitions (Moore/Zeller 2009: 109).

In *Bungalow Germania* the pavilion intersects with a partial replica of the *Kanzlerbungalow* in Bonn. The former German chancellor's official residence and workplace was built in 1964 by architect Sep Ruf, as Bonn was the capital of West Germany (»Kanzlerbungalow« n.d.). According to modernist American ideals, the building has transparency, clarity, and simplicity as its architectural language and is built with massive glass windows to view the wide vistas of its surroundings. Built to reflect a new democratic beginning, the *Kanzlerbungalow* was just as well raised on a political fundament. At the time of erection, West Germany strived to integrate the idea of the European welfare state along the lines of growth and collective prosperity. Just as much as it was the government's headquarters, the bungalow was framed as the »living room of the nation« in its branding to the public. Despite the democratic ideal of transparency and its living room metaphor, the building was

2.
Kanzlerbungalow, Bonn, 1979. © Bundesarchiv.

hidden away by the River Rhine with a facade inaccessible to the public. A defining feature of the building's function has, in this way, always been its circulation and reproduction through other public mediums. The building was defunctionalized and soon slipped into oblivion as Berlin became the capital of Germany in 1990 (Lehnerer/Ciriacidis 2014).

Originally built as the architectural answer to new ideals, the bungalow entered a phase in which its meaning was reformulated but it is now an officially listed building for its style and political history, and it is also a visitor attraction (Wüstenrot Stiftung 2005).

Both the German pavilion and *Kanzlerbungalow* were directly built to reflect German and West German national identity at two different points in history, and although different, to reflect political ideals. Having crossed the threshold of becoming historical, the buildings have gained the fragmentary quality of trace in the absence of their original context. Simultaneously however, they still possess their representational potency from the past. In the case of the German pavilion, to an extent where it is perceived as an unbroken signifier, where a demolition or change of the building would keep its political history at bay, the *Kanzlerbungalow*, on the other hand, has been actively chosen as a preserved object of heritage.

Most often used with two-dimensional mediums like photography and film, the installation of *Bungalow Germania* is a large-scale three-dimensional architectural montage. With its modernist simplicity and glass facades, the replica intersects with the bombastic white stone walls and high ceilings of the pavilion. Like a typical Venetian palazzo, the pavilion has its strongest footing under the façade. Going through the ten-meter-high portico of the pavilion, visitors are suddenly met by the bungalow's low and warm wooden ceiling. Placed on a podium, the pavilion offers the bungalow a strangely raised position from the ground, in this way disrupting the horizontal and harmonious simplicity of the bungalow, a building type alien to Venice (Lehnerer/Ciriacidis 2014). Moving further into the installation, the bungalow's central patio comes into view. Normally a space under the open sky, the patio has now been framed by the pavilion's high monumental roof, which in the montage becomes an exhibition space. Originally connotative of the ideal of transparency, the bungalow's famous wide panorama windows now offer a blocked vista; disrupted by the white stone walls of the pavilion, they have become an undetermined object (ibid.: 29). Iconic to the original *Kanzlerbungalow* is the fireplace which normally faces the living room with its back turning toward an outdoor area. In the installation it has likewise gained a central position, however it is fenced off by stone walls on one side and the central exhibition space on the other.

Not only do two buildings meet, but two types of space also intersect in the installation. One, intentionally massive and monumental, and the other, intimate and domestic with their respective material aesthetics of warm wood and clinical stone walls. Simultaneously, the two different architectures grant each other new properties. The monumental and vertical space of the pavilion has been granted a fireplace and cross-cut with wooden panels, and the panorama windows of the bungalow no longer offer a view, while the building's patio has a roof. In the montage the composite parts are identifiable while at the same time intersecting and layering, in this way disrupting the functions intended for the different architectural elements.

On a closer look, the installation is not only creating the fissures and ruptures of a montage, however. The neat arrangement and clear orchestration of lines also creates a strange harmony between the buildings. By having another piece of architecture built into it, the pavilion is not only a backdrop to exhibit art. In the montage, the pavilion itself becomes exhibited as a piece of architectural heritage, thereby reinforcing its political and historical dimensions. Likewise, the montage positions the *Kanzlerbungalow* in a broader history of ideologically connoted architecture, questioning the extent to which transparency in architecture equals democracy. In this case, montage produces a space which relentlessly alternates between contrast and unity, exhibiting architectural heritage in a way that points at the fragility of political narratives and their dependence on having a language in architecture. Through a strategy of juxtaposition, the porous nature of the relationship between materiality and meaning is thus foregrounded.

Through their past political use and in their separate form, the German pavilion and the Kanzlerbungalow arguably call for representational ways of making sense which Ben Anderson describes as meaning located in discourse, ideology or symbolic order (Anderson/Harrison 2010: 2). By positioning the buildings in a montage however, they create a representational void, turning each other into fragments of their original style and function. A third space is then created, which is more than the sum of its parts. It is a space where the experience of architecture arguably lends itself to a performative rather than representational elaboration.

3.
Alex Lehnerer and Savvas Ciriacidis: Bungalow Germania, Venice, Italy, 2014.
Photograph: Bas Princen.

4.
Alex Lehnerer and Savvas Ciriacidis: Bungalow Germania, Venice, Italy, 2014.
Photograph: Bas Princen.

5.
Alex Lehnerer and Savvas Ciriacidis: Bungalow Germania, Venice, Italy, 2014.
Photograph: Bas Princen.

From Grand Narratives to the Performative Fragment

The »performative« is a nomadic concept that generally refers to how meaning is specific to context and inseparable from the enactment of it. Nevertheless, the concept is anchored in J. L. Austin's conception of rhetorical performativity as put forth in his 1975 book *How to Do Things with Words*. Here, speech is suggested as inseparable from the social enactment of it, thereby stressing the social effect of the speech act itself (Austin 1971). Whereas performativity stems from the field of language and philosophy, the notion of performance stems from a theatrical understanding of performance as a scripted act (the dancer performs the choreographer's choreography). When talking about performance as connected to performativity however, it is not referring to representations of reality but rather as a creator and participant of reality. We perform acts in daily life and performance is therefore also connected to cultural rites and habits, and is a bodily and sensuous way of grasping the world (Phelan 1993: 146). The slippery and ephemeral nature of performance here leaves space for meaning to fluctuate and calls upon its spectator to grasp it.

With the so-called performative turn in the 1990s, the focus on the performative arose as a reaction against the explanation of social life through symbolic and textual representations (Dirksmeier/Helbrecht 2008: 1f). Similar to the idea that social identity, including gender, is produced through enactments in daily life, the performativity of architecture refers to how its meanings are created in moments of encounter (Butler 1990). Architects Helle Juul and Flemming Frost define the performative space as a »space of activity« contrasting what they call »representational space«. They sum up further: »The performative accordingly consists of *getting something to happen*, of providing the occasion for something to occur« (JUUL/FROST Architects 2011: 144). In her book *Uses of Heritage*, Laurajane Smith introduces the concept of performativity in relation to heritage. As she notes on performativity »it reinforces the idea that heritage is not a passive subject of management and conservation or tourist visitation – but rather an active process engaged with the construction and negotiation of meaning« (Smith 2006: 66).

Whether modern simplicity and democratic outlook or classical grandeur and subordination, the »complete« non-montaged versions of the German pavilion and the *Kanzlerbungalow* were both meant to represent political systems. Looking at the buildings separately their symbolism is clear. Indeed, they were also built to embody intentional architectural scripts for their users to enact. Approaching the German pavilion and entering its space, the visitor feels increasingly smaller. The scale is not human and a strange distance between building and visitor is created. Instead of being inclined to use the space actively, the vertical lines and the cool atmosphere makes the visitor look up and stand still. On the contrary, the *Kanzlerbungalow* immediately embraces its users with its earthy colors and materials. The body is invited to move around in the narrower corridors and spaces, and the fireplace offers a fixed point of orientation and the glass panels an outlook for a moment of reflection. Both buildings are also dependent on our bodily enactments of their architectural principles to sustain their representational power. As argued by architect and artist Vito Acconci, architecture is inherently a total-itarian activity, as the design of space is a manipulation of people's behavior (SHOWstudio 2012). In this sense, the buildings are architectural scripts for their users to perform.

By turning the two architectural languages into scripts with erasures in the montage, moments of uncertainty are produced. Which roof are we to orient ourselves toward? The bungalow's wooden one, or is this merely an exhibited piece under the real roof of the pavilion's exhibition? In the montage of Bungalow Germania we look up, through, and around, as an attempt to orient ourselves in the space. The glass panels which were meant to offer wide views and blur the division between the inside and outside, now mostly offer reflections of the visitors themselves. Metaphorically, this is telling for how the montage is an artistic strategy which actively points back at the interpreter to assign meaning to what has become fragmented. If architecture is essentially the totalitarian activity as suggested by Acconci here, montage is a way of engaging critically with this aspect, as it unfixes common readings and enactments of it. Through its simultaneous play on contrast and harmony, the montage of Bungalow Germania disrupts the representational power of the two buildings. This break in reproduction of the body releases a performative space to inhabit here. It is performative as it both addresses our unconscious expectations of space as regulated and simultaneously invites us to fill the representational void with new interpre-tations. By bringing the buildings together, they are accentuated as part of the same history of political architecture. As visitors, we are thus not only left to scrutinize the morals of having uncomfortable heritage in use but what exactly happens if this is erased or replaced. We are also made aware of the very hierarchization within this architectural history and how we ourselves are contributing to the selection of our built heritage at the expense of other buildings. This question is intrinsic to the *Kanzlerbungalow* itself; which fell into oblivion after the German capital was shifted from Bonn to Berlin in 1990 and its later reincarnation as an actively preserved heritage object for the public to visit.

Another performative layer of the montage is brought about by the *Kanzlerbungalow* being a partial replica. In the montage, the replica is not created as functional architecture but as a route to question its specific historical value. It is inserted in the montage as an associative space, redirecting a question of authenticity toward a reflection on how we value the building in a broader history of political architecture, and to what extent it can represent a collective identity. As it happens, the *Kanzlerbungalow* replica further inscribes itself into a history of iconic reproductions through other media representations of the building which defined public perception of it to a large extent. In this way, the Venetian replica is yet another performative gesture of the original bungalow in Bonn; in this case questioning its political message through its juxtaposition with the pavilion.

6.
Ludwig Wegmann: Kanzlerbungalow, Bonn, 1972.
»The nation's living room« gained a public life through photographs.
Coalition talks between the Social Democratic Party of Germany (SPD) and the
Free Democratic Party (FDP) in the chancellor's bungalow.

Being planned as an exhibition, the montage of Bungalow Germania is itself a designed and scripted space within the frames of the Biennale. However, in planning with a release of a conceptual layer which can only be filled out by the perceiving body to define, the montage becomes a principle of preservation by which architectural heritage is not merely passed on to future generations. Rather, the historical object comes forth in the figure of the fragment, inviting us to perform a question regarding our faith in representations as markers of collective identity. Although clashing with architectural language and in combining site-specificity with an uprooted version of a building, the third space created evokes an uncanny experience of how seemingly mutually exclusive spaces are interrelated, just as we thought they were not. This is even more interesting considering how modern architecture and the early writings of the modern movement singled out monumental architecture and its »permanent representation of power in any form« as its biggest opponent (Kamleithner 2014: 165). Encountering the buildings in their fragmentation and overlapping thus seems a reminder of the latent instability of architectural representations at any given time, as they are caught up in a symbiotic relationship to maintain their representational order and hierarchization. By exhibiting the buildings as part of the same architectural history, we are invited to enact the transitional condition of ontological uncertainty that all buildings now perceived as »historical« have experienced at some point. As an experimental principle of preservation, montage thus offers architectural heritage as a mode of negotiation, more than something which is passed on and either protected or discarded.

Architectural Montage as Experimental Preservation

In the case of Bungalow Germania, montage is an experimental preservationist intervention which moves architectural heritage from a representational to a performative mode of being. The result is heritage experienced as a third space in which historical meanings not easily dissolved into the grand narratives of 20th-century German and European ideologies are negotiated. Whereas preservation often serves to retain an object's original substance and idea, the montage however, recontextualizes and distances the buildings from their original settings and meanings. Strangely enough, this somehow brings the buildings closer to the visitor as they address our own expectations and bodily enactments of them.

Here, working with the performative is a way to bring an experiential aspect to preservation, turning heritage into something that we practice in context more than objects we merely have (Smith 2006). In juxtaposing the two heritage objects, the boundaries between the actual representative potency of each building and the very process of exhibiting architecture are dissolved; adding an irony to the installation (Lehnerer/Ciriacidis 2014). That we are faced with a replica, frustrates the element of authenticity as one of the cornerstones of conventional preservation even more. Within this understanding, a copy would often be perceived as a violation of the original and its *real* historical significance, which aligns with the replica's status as tacky or even »camp« within popular culture (Engel 2018). Being objects of preservation that are certainly canonical and part of an official heritage discourse, the montage rather underlines both buildings as an existential condition, whether we accept them or not. From there, the question about the extent to which history and national identity can be accessed through historical architecture emerges. As an experimental preservationist approach, intervention here tests our relation to the heritage object more than it reaffirms it. It becomes clear however, that no specific story is told; also bringing an odd simplicity to the installation and the easily read architectural languages of the bungalow and pavilion respectively. What remains is how relevant the architectural montage is to formulating questions through spatial and bodily means. In the case of Bungalow Germania, montage provides a reading of highly representational architecture through performative means in which heritage becomes an object of negotiation through different modes of architectural being. The discursive element of the montage in interrupting established order leaves us with the question of what meaning architecture holds when its functions and embedded metaphors are disturbed. The combination of two known entities results in what Eisenstein referred to as »Tertium Quid« – a third indefinite whole bigger than the sum of its parts (Gullström 2010: 28). In the architectural montage of Bungalow Germania this becomes an experimental principle of preservation – preservation not only when dealing with culturally significant objects, but itself becoming a self-reflexive and culturally significant practice.

References

Anderson, Ben/Harrison, Paul (2010): Taking-Place: *Non-Representational Theories and Geography*, Abingdon: Routledge.

Association of Critical Heritage Studies: »History«, https://www.criticalheritagestudies.org/history, accessed October 6, 2021.

Austin, John L. (1971): *How to Do Things with Words*, London: Oxford University Press.

Benjamin, Walter (2002): *Arcades Project*, revised edition, Cambridge, MA/London: Harvard University Press.

Butler, Judith (1990): *Gender Trouble: Feminism and the Subversion of Identity*, New York: Routledge.

Dirksmeier, Peter/Helbrecht, Ilse (2008): »Time, non-representational theory and the ›performative turn‹ – towards a new methodology in qualitative social research«, in: *The Forum: Qualitative Social Research, vol. 9, no. 2*, 1–15.

Druckrey, Timothy (1994): »From Dada to Digital: Montage in the Twentieth Century«, in: *Aperture, Summer 1994*, 4–7.

Eisenstein, Sergei M. (1989 [1937–1940]): »Montage and Architecture«, transl. by Michael Glenny, in: *Assemblage 10*, 111–131. https://doi.org/10.2307/3171145

Engel, Barbara (ed.) (2018): *Historisch versus modern: Identität durch Imitat?* – English translation: *Historical versus Modern: Identity through Imitation?*, Berlin: JOVIS.

Gullström, Charlie (2010): *Presence Design: Mediated Spaces Extending Architecture*, doctoral thesis, Stockholm: Department of Architecture, Royal Institute of Technology (KTH), https://www.diva-portal.org/smash/get/diva2:349960/FULLTEXT01.pdf, accessed November 18, 2022.

Haus der Geschichte Bonn (n.d.): »Kanzlerbungalow 1964–1999«, https://www.hdg.de/haus-der-geschichte/historische-orte/kanzlerbungalow, accessed August 30, 2021.

Heilmeyer, Florian (2014): »The Unhappy Nation: The Trouble with the German Pavilion«, in: *uncube, Blog Venice 2014*, http://www.uncubemagazine.com/blog/13419027, accessed August 30, 2021.

JUUL/FROST Architects (2011): *Public Space 2: The Familiar into the Strange [Byens rum 2 – Det kendte i det fremmede]*, transl. by Dan A. Marmorstein, Copenhagen, http://byensrum.dk/english/documents/PublicSpace2.pdf, accessed November 18, 2022.

Kamleithner, Christa (2014): »What Architecture Does«, in: *Get Real! Architectural Realities, ARCH+ 217*, Aachen: ARCH+ Verlag GmbH, 156–169.

Lehnerer, Alex/Ciriacidis, Savvas (eds.) (2014): *Bungalow Germania: German Pavilion – 14th International Architecture Exhibition la Biennale di Venezia 2014*, Ostfildern: Hatje Cantz Verlag.

Moore, Elke/Zeller, Ursula (2009): *Germany's Contributions to the Venice Biennale 1885–2007*, Cologne: Dumont Buchverlag.

Newman, Michael (1989): »Revising Modernism, Representing Postmodernism«, in: Lisa Appignanesi (ed.): *Postmodernism: Institute of Contemporary Arts Documents*, London: Free Association Books, 95–154.

Oelze, Sabine (2011): »Germany's Pavilion at the Venice Biennale Can't Escape History«, https://www.dw.com/en/curators-split-over-fate-of-germanys-nazi-era-pavilion-at-venice-biennale/a-5754228, accessed August 30, 2021.

Otero-Pailos, Jorge/Langdalen, Erik Fenstad
Langdalen/Arrhenius, Thordis (eds.) (2016):
Experimental Preservation, Zurich: Lars Müller
Publishers.

Paterson, Tony (2010): »Calls for demolition
of ›Nazi‹ pavilion in Venice«, https://
www.independent.co.uk/news/world/
europe/calls-demolition-nazi-pavilion-
venice-2020066.html, accessed August 30,
2021.

Phelan, Peggy (1993): *Unmarked: The Politics
of Performance*, Abingdon: Routledge.

SHOWstudio (2012): »In Your Face: Interview,
Vito Acconci«, https://www.showstudio.
com/projects/in_your_face_interviews/
vito_acconci, accessed November 18, 2022.

Smith, Laurajane (2006): *Uses of Heritage*,
New York: Routledge.

Sperling, Joshua/Barndt, Kerstin/Kriebel,
Sabine (2016): »Montage«, in: *Routledge
Encyclopedia of Modernism*, London:
Routledge, doi: 10.4324/9781135000356-
REMO18-1

Wüstenrot Stiftung (2005): *Kanzlerbungalow
in Bonn*, https://wuestenrot-stiftung.de/
kanzlerbungalow-sep-ruf-bonn/, accessed
August 30, 2021.

PERCEPTION

»If one thinks of the montage process as the application of a visual grammar in order to compose narratives, then paths work as verbs.«

Erieta Attali: *Montage: From Images to Narratives, p.130.*

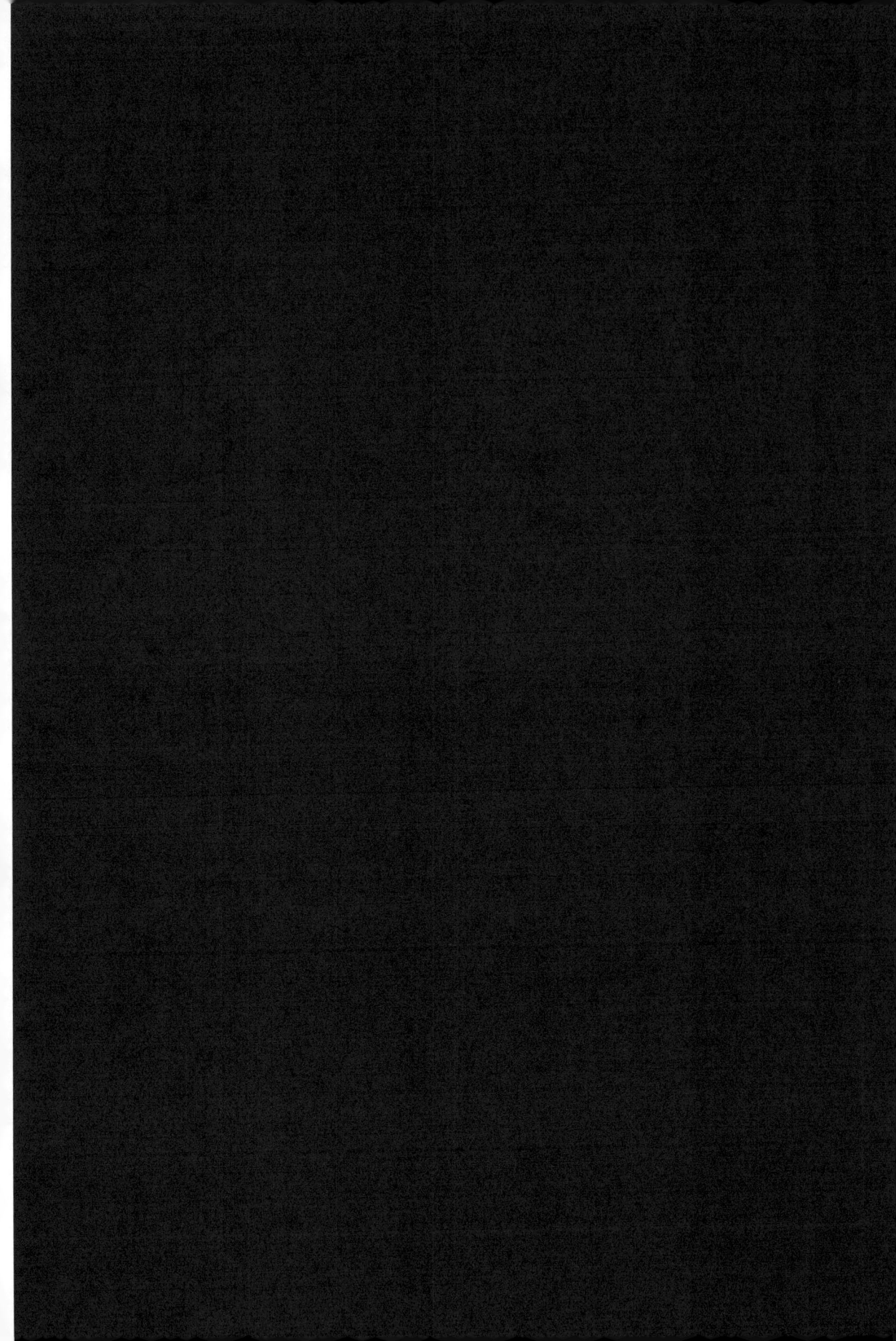

Dimensions. Journal of Architectural Knowledge, 2022-04 ⑧
https://doi.org/10.14361/dak-2022-0412

Montages in Mind
On the Formative Role of Perceivers in Architecture

Julian Franke

Abstract: Perceiving the built environment is not only based on physical, material objects, and sensory stimuli but consists of numerous aspects and levels of consciousness. Among others, memories of previous experiences, expectations, desires or inclinations are imaginatively brought into our perception and linked in a formative way. Therefore, immaterial and imaginary levels of mind are equally relevant to the reception and interpretation of architecture. This paper highlights the characteristics of these processes of perception in which all fragments of consciousness are combined as strikingly similar to montage techniques. The collecting, arranging, and assembling of certain heterogeneous fragments can also be found in the human mind, since single sensual and mental fragments are mounted to a continuous flow and harmonious whole. This text aims to emphasize the importance of *mental montages* in daily life and to widen the understanding of concepts of time and space, as well as of reality and actuality in the perception of architecture. Consequently, architecture is not only physically built but also mentally constructed, which is why perceivers should be respected as creators of their own environment and actuality.

Keywords: Association; Experience; Imagination; Interpretation; Memory; Mental Constructivism; Perception; Temporality.

Corresponding author: Julian Franke (Lucerne University of Applied Sciences and Arts, Switzerland);
franke.architektur@gmail.com; http://orcid.org/0000-0003-3581-0364

Introduction

»After all, people don't live in piles of bricks, but in spaces of imagination and landscapes of memory« (Brock 2008: 37, author's translation).

In everyday life, many people encounter numerous buildings, public spaces or other spatial situations and perceive them consciously or unconsciously while moving through the built environment. In this process, the human senses are stimulated by the environment which are interpreted to create meaning. However, the built environment is not only accessed with the senses via sensory stimuli, but also intellectually, through interpretations along architectural signs, including experiences that one has made and stored, such as memories. Thus, one always brings something imaginary into perception.

The process of perception is complex and consists of numerous aspects and levels of consciousness. Besides the mentioned memories of previous experiences, one carries expectations, desires, inclinations, and much more. Therefore, perception is not only based on the physically present but is equally shaped by immaterial, imaginary levels of mind that are above all formative so that the material world seems to change on the basis of (inter) subjective constructions. These implementations of levels of consciousness, these additions, arrangements, and links to different experiences or ideas will be considered in the following text as a form of montage that is essential to the perception and creation of architecture.

Montage is a process of collecting, arranging, and assembling certain heterogeneous materials or fragments that were once separated in time and space. The chosen parts are inserted into an existing situation in such a way that something »new« is created from these fragments. Even though the original characteristics of the assembled elements remain identifiable in the new composition, the arrangement as a whole creates a new meaning that overwrites its origin and blurs the intersections. It can be noted that the characteristics of montage are mainly based on acts of editing and producing in relation to images, texts or materials, while those of perceptual processes consist of mental images, language, and sensuality. In the mind, too, single sensual and mental fragments appear as a continuous flow and harmonious whole since their transitions also seem to blur.

Theorists and authors from the world of philosophy, psychology, and architecture will be re-introduced to this text to widen the understanding of montage techniques beyond physical, artistic acts such as in photography, design or filmmaking, and to highlight the importance of *mental montages* in daily life – especially those within the built environment. Through this mental ability, all perceivers create their own reality via their formative imagination and mounted experiences. It is necessary to consider the role of montage in the context of architectural perception and to highlight that architecture is not only physically built but also mentally constructed and respectively mounted in every single moment.

Montages of Experiences

Since Immanuel Kant's epistemology, in the context of his *Critique of Pure Reason*, and the constructivism in philosophy – for example by Ernst von Glasersfeld or Heinz von Foerster – as well as in psychology – for example by Jean Piaget or Paul Watzlawick with his question »how real is real?« (Watzlawick 1977) – it has been widely accepted that humans have no pure perception of the world or of an object as a *thing-in-itself* (Kant 1999 [1781]). On the one hand, perception is limited and filtered by the sensual apparatus, by language and social interdependencies, and on the other it is influenced and enhanced by the perceivers in a creative, constructive way. It is also enhanced by individual, differently made and stored experiences which are brought sometimes more, sometimes less effectively into the present perception. Imaginations and interpretations, as well as expectations of the future affect access to the (built) environment considerably. As a result, humans not only find themselves in certain realities or worlds; they also create them.

In his semiotic work on the presence of signs in architecture, architectural theorist Jörg Gleiter identifies that architectural experience consists of a combination of sensual perception and mental apperception. He concludes that architecture is – despite its physical presence – always the object of an imagination and consciousness that goes beyond what is currently perceptible through the senses (Gleiter 2014: 150). Architect and theorist Elisabeth Blum stresses that spatial perception is not neutral but highly productive, sometimes furiously fast or sometimes contemplatively slow, and can cause surprise by being unpredictable.

Furthermore, she describes how productive spatial perception as montage is not plannable and instead happens uncontrollably or unconsciously (Blum 2010: 11). However, this imaginary element should not be taken too negatively: To be able to recognize at all, everything must make sense in the perception and thus be associated with something. To perceive and understand, connections must be made with associations that are in alignment with stored experiences. The psychologist Alexandra Abel points out that imagination is essential in order to perceive and understand the environment, whether as an impression, mere hunch or word. One must possess a conception of it (Abel 2018: 28).

Perception is therefore shaped not only by long-past experiences that are brought in imaginatively, but also by those that are caught consciously or unconsciously immediately before, for example on the way to a building. This is why the Swiss sociologist and planning theorist Lucius Burckhardt speaks in his work on »strollology«, developed in the 1980s, of a flow of perception as a concatenation of impressions in successive places that shape perceivers in the way they will perceive what follows. He emphasizes that the journey to a building, park or landscape is already formative, and not only the individual places themselves, whereby »the path is the goal«. The collection of impressions on a walk is important, above all because, according to Burckhardt, humans do not perceive like parachutists who land at certain places but are decisively influenced by the previous way (Burckhardt 2015: 225). The aforementioned concatenation, a sequence or chain of impressions which then endures in further perceptions, he also recalls a string of pearls which, on the one hand has more expressive and on the other, less expressive passages but always effective passages that synthesize one's perception (ibid.: 290).

This understanding of influential experiences as a sequence or juxtaposition of different perspectives on the paths through the built environment identifies characteristics of chronological time sequences that seem comparable to montage techniques of filmmaking. In the following however, this text aims to highlight the compatibility of perception with montage techniques, such as in photography – for example, the intersection and superimposition of images – where time and space merge in one perception as a montage of actual sensual stimuli and experiences previously collected through immaterial imagination.

When standing in front of a building and viewing it, imagination overlaps with the received sensual stimuli and can even partly overwrite them: an intertwining of seeing the material environment and the immaterial content of mind. Finnish architect Juhani Pallasmaa points out that when observing the environment both states must be taken into account: »We need to acknowledge that we live in mental and fundamentally subjective worlds of memory, dream and imagination as much as in a perceived material, physical and experientially shared world. Paradoxically, our world is given to us, but at the same time, it is of our own making« (Pallasmaa 2011: 36).

However, both states start from the same objects. The perception refers to real, physical objects while imaginations or memories are based on the imprints of these perceptions. On the one hand, the balance of more material or immaterial aspects can result unconsciously, yet it can also be a conscious decision whether to focus more on perception or more on imagining in a specific moment. The impression is that people are able to focus more on the facts of the present at one time and more on the remnants of the past at another. In this process, the origins of perception often can't be distinguished anymore when the transitions between them are blurred.

In his work on visual thinking, the theorist and perceptual psychologist, Rudolf Arnheim, clarifies that there can be no decision between a pure perception or a pure conception. He therefore explains that they are complementary. He points out that the images of memories influence and complete the perception, and that one can't distinguish between a »pure« perceptual image and one based on memory. Likewise, memories also don't emerge without a present flow of perception (Arnheim 1980 [1972]: 88). The fragments of a mental montage blur into each other, almost like superimpositions of transparent images that redefine background and foreground and create something new, while the single elements stay evident.

Montages of Associations and Interpretations

As previously indicated, experiences and memories are an essential part of the imaginative contribution toward our perception. For Swiss architect Peter Zumthor, working with atmospheric and remembered images of his experiences is a key element of his work. Thus, »associative, wild, free, ordered and systematic thinking in images, in architectural, spatial, colorful and sensuous pictures« is his favorite definition and preferred origin of designing methods (Zumthor 1999: 59). By working extensively with images of memory, he has a special relationship to the past. That is why he high-lights the importance of the past, in which he sees that all feeling and under-standing is rooted. Therefore, one's sensuous connection to, and creation of meaning in, a building should respect the process of remembering (Zumthor 1999: 18).

In this sense, one should also assume that memory is necessary. The German sociologist Harald Welzer, for example, regards it as an orientation aid for the present. According to Welzer, one makes use of the past through memory stocks in a utilitarian and opportunistic way. Leftover fragments of expe-riences are assembled in specific ways and then it is checked whether the assembly works in aiding orientation. If the arrangement turns out to be too conflictual, it is reorganized until it is arranged – we could say mounted – in a way that promotes agreement and functionality (Welzer 2005: 34).

This use of archived fragments is similar to the technique of montage in photography, where photographs or single pieces are also taken from an archive. A person's archive is a kind of photo album or picture gallery that consists of either concrete or sketchy impressions as imprints of what was once seen or experienced. According to Blum, these mental images can have multiple sources; they may even come from several worlds. For example, these can be: real three-dimensional spatial situations; associations; memo-ries or forms of knowledge (Blum 2010: 11).

Especially if one cannot initially recognize or understand an object or building, the fragments of one's archive have an importance for making own associations that can lead to interpretations and better understanding. For example, Arnheim clarifies that one relies upon experiences and memories even more if a given object is so ambiguous and difficult to interpret that one starts searching for the most appropriate model based on the differently stored shapes and images in one's memory (Arnheim 1980 [1972]: 93). The less one can understand or categorize the objects of an environment, the more one tries to explain that environment intellectually based on the differently mounted knowledge and memories. This is comparable to Welzer's theory that in the search for the most suitable model for one's understanding and orientation, one extracts missing parts from oneself.

This searching and associating for meaning becomes understandable, espe-cially in relation to the work of the philosopher, Ludwig Wittgenstein. He explains that humans can perceive the environment once as one thing and once as another thing, while the way it is seen is based on how it is interpreted (Wittgenstein 2009: 203e). Perception is similarly an interpretive seeing that is dynamic and dependent on personal choice or focus. Wittgenstein also calls this the »seeing-as«, which is based on noticing different aspects of an object or image and depends upon what either attracts the senses and links with one's knowledge or what is consciously focused upon. According to him, the seeing-as »is not part of perception. And therefore, it is like seeing, and again not like seeing« (ibid.: 207e), it is rather an intellectual act. The philosopher Gunter Gebauer argues that the recipient takes the initiative by this seeing-as and is thus in a creatively acting role (Gebauer 2010: 82). It becomes clearer how the creative character of interpretive perception through mental montages prevents humans from a pure perception. However, without the mounted levels, one would only be confronted by an indefinable, unrecognizable mass of material.

In the manner of constructivism, the perspectival, interpretive character of perception inevitably questions a single world; a single reality that humans live in. On the contrary, humans generate a multiplicity of possible meanings, realities or even worlds. »We are not speaking in terms of multiple possible alternatives to a single actual world but of multiple actual worlds« as Nelson Goodman explains (Goodman 1978: 2). Building on Goodman's work *Ways of Worldmaking*, the German philosopher Günter Abel clarifies that every experience made could also be different. A multiplicity of possible causes of an experience can legitimately be assumed and they depend on individually found aspects and interpretations. According to Abel, humans have opinions, beliefs, and justifiable knowledge based on formed worlds that result from their own interpretation processes. He defines these as processes in which one phenomenally discriminates against something as a certain thing and then identifies and re-identifies it, applies properties and labels, attributes something to it, and divides and classifies it, as well as constructs relations to it. Therefore, the formed worlds humans live in can be qualified as *worlds of interpretation* (Abel 1993: 14) and the processes used to construct them share several characteristics with the definition of montage. This becomes even more obvious when Abel writes about processes of interpretive perceiving, such as spatio-temporal arrangements, exclusions, preferences or the categorization of specific elements, as well as complementary additions or erasures (ibid.: 270). It follows that the individual handling of certain elements based on experiences forms one's interpretations, constructs new contexts, and thus forms other worlds or realities.

Yet, for all the subjectivity of these individually assembled realities, it is still important to assume a kind of objectivity or intersubjectivity in perception. Humans can share communication and exchanges about the same things in the world, and they can compare or be influenced by the same things in similar ways. In this sense, the sculptor Axel Seyler points out that there is no purely subjective perception at all, which would then also be called something completely different. For him, the main problem of a purely subjective perception is that one could not talk about the visible forms of the environment (Seyler 2018: 129). That is comparable with the impossibility of using a private language in Wittgenstein's philosophical investigations. Perceptions are therefore merely subjectively shaped but intersubjectively comprehensible.

Another fundamental form of mental montage can be found in the work of philosopher Edmund Husserl. He highlights that an object never falls into one's perception in its complete appearance from all sides, with all its sensual peculiarities, no matter how perfect one's perception might be (Husserl 2007: 165). Thus, one always sees only a single side when it is viewed from the front, two sides when it is viewed from perspective or three sides when viewed, for example, from the underside of an elevated structure or from above. According to Husserl, perception is thus always imperfect and only grasps something of an object, while it also reaches into a void that wants to be filled. What seems to be known, Husserl considers as always being partly unknown. As such, for him, all certain knowledge seems hopeless from the beginning (ibid.: 180).

Even though only little is given by an object or building, one does not see a lone standing »wall« or a single »façade« in an architectural elevation but a »building« as a whole; as a complete object. According to Husserl, one refers to the visible, partially given properties and applies information to the other not given parts in such a way that these are considered as not given but as still belonging to the same object (ibid.: 166). Therefore, the missing invisible properties and parts – such as other façades – are required by the recipient in the mind. They are also presented as assumptions in the interpretation and understanding of the visible, and as filling the perceptual voids.

Montages of Space and Time

It has become clear so far that temporality – at least in the form of the past (memories/experiences) and present (current sensory stimuli/interpretations) – takes on a particularly large role in the context of mental montages. Therefore, time plays a two-fold role: Each perception itself exists as a flow of varying fragments in a temporal sequence that one cannot stop while the collected elements of mental montages are also rooted in different times. Elisabeth Blum sees a specific property of spatial perception in the interplay of the durable, permanent character of real space and the fleeting nature of one's associative mental montages. Thus, the stable space begins to multiply and change by invisible dimensions as soon as humans enter it (Blum 2010: 12).

Besides the past and the present, however, it is also important to consider the future. Relevant expectations and plans for action in the future are brought into perception and decisively determine how certain parts are related to each other, and how objects are seen. Prejudices become assumptions and expectations about what we might find in a building, what usually happens in such a place, what one wants from it, and are superimposed and mounted respectively in one's perception as well. An anticipation of the future is also an elementary component of a feeling of orientation and supposedly prepares us for the unpredictable. Humans do not only live in landscapes of memory, they also live one step ahead in the future.

In addition to the aspects of temporality, the mounting of spatial aspects is also significant and makes space appear relative. Experiences made in other places, derivations of other epochs in other regions, or the specific atmospheres of certain places have an effect on perception and those perceiving. Architecture is again not only the assembly of individual components, but the experience of social, regional or foreign elements brought and mounted together in mind. Humans are able, even if only physically present in one place at a time, to construct a superimposition of various places, buildings, and cities in one place through a mental montage technique so that a new place is constructed within them. »We transfer all the cities and towns that we have visited, all the places that we have recognized, into the incarnate memory of our body. Our domicile becomes integrated with our self-identity; it becomes part of our own body and being« (Pallasmaa 2005: 72).

Blum highlights the demand of exchange for the constructivist character of the perceiving – or rather reading – of places. She mentions the linking of elements from far-distant places and realities as an almost deconstructivist disassembly of what belonged together with a reinsertion of individual parts elsewhere. Thus, hard facts, fragments, memories, and imaginations can be understood as the building blocks of mental constructions (Blum 2010: 125). Even without extensive knowledge of architecture, humans can recognize aspects of *Bauhausstil* in different countries, identify a Roman bath even though it is in a British city or find aspects of a Greek temple in the Neue Nationalgalerie in Berlin by Mies van der Rohe. Once collected impressions from another place or based on photographs in different media expand one's knowledge and fill the individual archives. These can then be deconstructed in another context for further comparisons and interpretations.

Can one still speak of a reality at all if the world is mounted by humans through both subjective and intersubjective imaginary constructions? In the context of aesthetics, philosopher Gernot Böhme distinguishes between the concepts of *actuality* and *reality* which are directly linked to human perception. According to him, actuality is what is given in our current perception and is likewise dependent on each perceiver. Besides that, the real or reality is what may materially form the basis of each actuality but independent from the perceivers (Böhme 2001: 57). Thus, one receives stimuli from the real things around which are perceived as an actuality that is mediated by one's senses and intellectual interpretations. Art theorist William John Thomas Mitchell makes a similar distinction in his image theory. He separates the seeing that can be understood as an image of mere information on the retina from the individual seeing that constitutes the identity of the observer. Here, too, an understanding of reality and actuality can be read out. Mitchell calls the first type of vision the information transmitting »bodily eye« – which corresponds to reality – and the second type the individual, interpreting »mental eye« – which corresponds to actuality (Mitchell 1994: 51). With the concept of the mental eye, he also brings in the level of imagination which was introduced in this text as mental montage shaping the human's actualities and (inter)subjectively created worlds. Reality, on the other hand, comprises matter which often remains rather unchanged despite all its many interpretations and meanings can change.

Conclusion

It was shown that human perception is influenced by many factors and is always predetermined and constructed. Consciously or unconsciously made experiences are imaginatively mounted into perception. Besides individual characteristics of sensory perception associations and interpretations make the perceiver the creator of his own reality, or better said actuality. Thus, one's understanding of the (built) environment is not only dependent on real, physical qualities of objects, but in particular also on the immaterial levels of imagination, which are brought along and assembled with the current sensual stimuli. Without imaginations, perception would be poorer or even impossible. Moreover, perception is as spontaneous, vivid and dynamic as life itself. Human does not perceive contextless single objects in his environment, but a world as an interrelated network, which, as a mounted whole, depends on (inter)subjective experiences or actions. With Pallasmaa can be summarized: »A building is a structure of utility, matter and construction, as well as an imaginary spatiotemporal metaphor for a better world. Artistic and architectural works exist thus in the realms of physics and metaphysics, reality and fiction, construction and image, use and desire, all at the same time« (Pallasmaa 2011: 93).

The mental montage is not only a juxtaposition of impressions and situations like in film, but, in particular, also a merge of the imaginary and the sensual as a superimposition in one moment and place, comparable with photomontage. Perception, thus, covers the temporal sequence of long past memories, immediately preceding experiences as well as the current perception itself and the future related anticipations of the not (yet) existent. Nevertheless, every imagination is grounded in the past, in that it does not bring forth anything fundamentally new but works with the accumulated impressions of previous life.

Imagination and interpretation must be taken into account, because only through them meaning is created beyond the sensory stimuli one receives. The explained mental montages contribute to the fact that the physical world can change also non-physically, what leads to the conclusion that also perceivers should be respected as creators of architecture and urban spaces, which should not be planned for architects, but for the perceiving users and recipients.

182   Julian Franke

References

Abel, Alexandra (2018): »Architektur und Aufmerksamkeit« (»Architecture and Attention«), in: Alexandra Abel/Bernd Rudolf (eds.), *Architektur wahrnehmen (Perceiving Architecture)*, Bielefeld: transcript Verlag, 21–50, doi: 10.14361/9783839436547-003

Abel, Günter (1993): *Interpretationswelten: Gegenwartsphilosophie jenseits von Essentialismus und Relativismus (Worlds of Interpretation: Contemporary Philosophy beyond Essentialism and Relativism)*, Frankfurt a. M.: Suhrkamp.

Arnheim, Rudolf (1980 [1972]): *Anschauliches Denken: Zur Einheit von Bild und Begriff (Visual Thinking: On the Unity of Image and Concept)*, Köln: DuMont Buchverlag.

Blum, Elisabeth (2010): *Atmosphäre: Hypothesen zum Prozess der räumlichen Wahrnehmung (Atmosphere: Hypotheses on the Process of Spatial Perception)*, Köln: Lars Müller Publishers.

Böhme, Gernot (2001): *Aisthetik: Vorlesungen über Ästhetik als allgemeine Wahrnehmungslehre (Aisthetics: Lectures on Aesthetics as General Theory of Perception)*, München: Fink.

Brock, Bazon (2008): *Lustmarsch durchs Theoriegelände – Musealisiert Euch! (Pleasure March through the Theoretical Terrain – Musealize yourselves!)*, Köln: DuMont.

Burckhardt, Lucius (2015): *Why Is Landscape Beautiful?: The Science of Strollology*, edited by Markus Ritter/Martin Schmitz, Basel: Birkhäuser.

Gebauer, Gunter (2010): »Sich-Zeigen und Sehen als: Wittgensteins zwei Bildkonzepte« (»Showing-itself and seeing as: Wittgenstein's two concepts of picture«), in: Gottfried Boehm/Sebastian Egenhofer/Christian Spies (eds.), *Zeigen: Die Rhetorik des Sichtbaren (Showing: The Rhetoric of the Visible)*, Lindenberg: Fink, 75–89, doi: 10.30965/9783846750094_005

Gleiter, Jörg H. (2014): »Präsenz der Zeichen: Vorüberlegungen zu einer phänomenologischen Semiotik der Architektur« (»Presence of signs: Preliminary Reflections on Phenomenological Semiotics of Architecture«), in: Jörg H. Gleiter (ed.), *Symptom Design: Vom Zeigen und Sich-Zeigen der Dinge (Symptom Design: On the Showing and Showing-itself of the things)*, Bielefeld: transcript Verlag, doi: 10.14361/transcript.9783839422687.148

Goodman, Nelson (1978): *Ways of Worldmaking (Harvester Studies in Philosophy)*, Hassocks: The Harvester Press.

Husserl, Edmund (2007): »Analyse der Wahrnehmung« (»Analysis of Perception«), in: Thomas Friedrich/Jörg H. Gleiter (eds.): *Einfühlung und phänomenologische Reduktion: Grundlagentexte zu Architektur, Design und Kunst (Empathy and Phenomenological Reduction: Foundational Texts on Architecture, Design, and Art)*, Münster: LIT Verlag, 165–181.

Kant, Immanuel (1999[1781]): *Critique of Pure Reason [Kritik der reinen Vernunft]*, edited by Paul Guyer/Allen W. Woods, Cambridge: Cambridge University Press.

Mitchell, William John Thomas (1994): *Picture Theory: Essays on Verbal and Visual Representation*, Chicago: University of Chicago Press.

Pallasmaa, Juhani (2011): *The Embodied Image: Imagination and Imagery in Architecture*, Chichester: John Wiley & Sons Ltd.

Pallasmaa, Juhani (2005): *The Eyes of the Skin: Architecture and the Senses*, Chichester: John Wiley & Sons Ltd.

Seyler, Axel (2018): »Förderer der Schönheit« (»Promoters of Beauty«), in: Alexandra Abel/ Bernd Rudolf (eds.), *Architektur wahrnehmen (Perceiving Architecture)*, Bielefeld: transcript Verlag, 123–152, doi: 10.14361/9783839436547-006

Watzlawick, Paul (1977): *How Real is Real?: Confusion, Disinformation, Communication*, New York: Vintage Books.

Welzer, Harald (2005): »Wozu erinnern wir uns? Einige Fragen an die Geschichtswissenschaften« (»What are we Remembering for? Some Questions for the Historical Sciences«), in: *Österreichische Zeitschrift für Geschichtswissenschaften (ÖZG)* 16/1:, 12–35, https://journals.univie.ac.at/index.php/oezg/article/view/4123/3884, accessed October 15, 2022.

Wittgenstein, Ludwig (2009): *Philosophical Investigations*, transl. by Gertrude E. M. Anscombe/Peter M. S. Hacker/Joachim Schulte, edited by Peter M. S. Hacker/Joachim Schulte, Chichester: Wiley-Blackwell.

Zumthor, Peter (1999): *Thinking Architecture*, Basel: Birkhäuser.

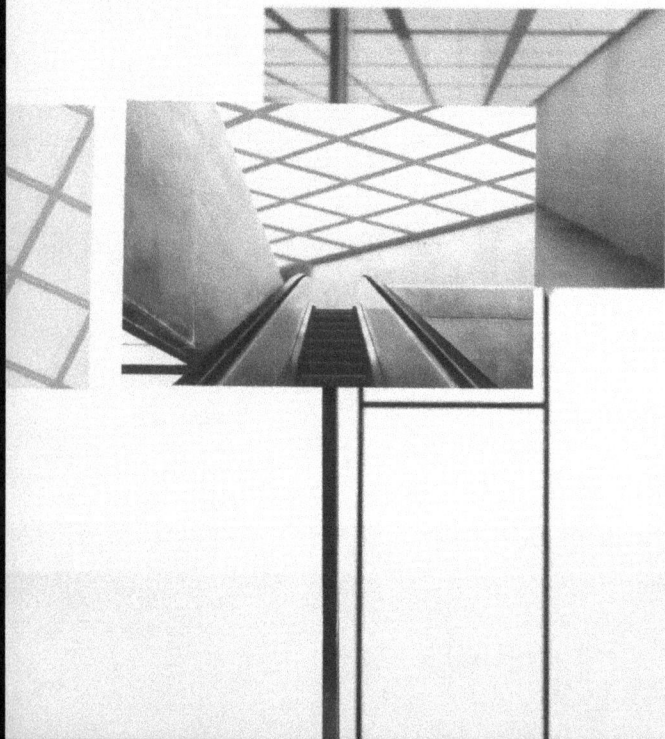

1.
Nils Fröhling: Paintings from the series »Qualities of Space«.
Prints on wooden plates mounted on metal poles, Munich, 2021.

Dimensions. Journal of Architectural Knowledge, 2022-04 ∂
https://doi.org/10.14361/dak-2022-0413

Qualities of Space
The Montage of Space in Painting

Nils Fröhling

Abstract: This article illuminates the thoughts and influences behind a series of paintings of imaginary architecture created between 2020 and 2021. It is an attempt to reveal some of the ideas, affinities, interests, and feelings montaged into these spatial environments. It sheds light on the theoretical context as well as on practical aspects of painting and the transformation of thoughts into images of spaces.

Keywords: Artistic Reflection; Metropolis; Painting; Perception of Space; Representation of Space; Speed; Technology.

Corresponding authors: Nils Fröhling (Technical University, Munich);
nils.froehling@icloud.com; https://orcid.org/0000-0002-6941-782X

2.

Paradoxically, it is precisely the anonymized, location-independent interiors of trains that make it possible to isolate temporary private spaces from them. While trains cross territorial boundaries at high speed, within them, the appropriation of private spaces is continually renegotiated. Digitally painted, 841 x 594mm.

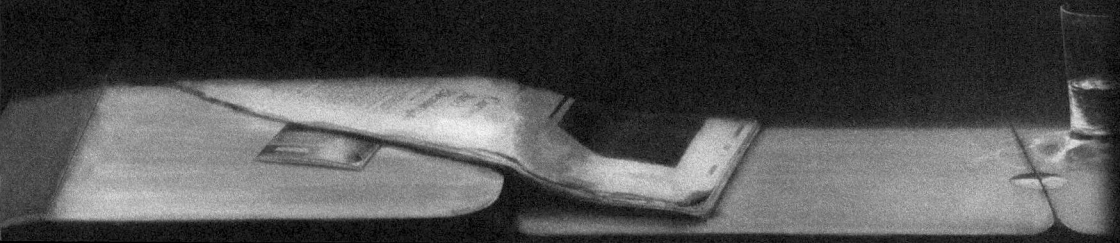

3.
The presence of images. Digitally painted, 841 x 594mm, 2021.

Context

For centuries, city walls have marked the boundaries between the urban realm and the countryside. Thereby, these physical borders clearly expressed the significant role for the establishment of spatial order through architectural means. Today, this dominance is called into question. When reading the transportation plans of present-day metropolises, this physical demarcation between the city and its surroundings is no longer visible. While the names of the individual subway stations are still a reminder of this urban heritage, no further indication exists in these representations of the urban space, neither the spatial boundaries and limits within a city nor any kind of physical border around the city are reflected. Although even the indicated cardinal directions of traffic lines do not perfectly correspond with the physical conditions, these plans are the most important orientation tool for traveling through a metropolis. Whereas they provide a sense of the temporal distances between individual places, they paradoxically express a distortion, a loss of the spatial sequences between adjacent places, and a blurring of formerly important architectural and territorial boundaries. What they reveal is that systems which are necessary to navigate the urban environment heavily influence the perception of urban space. It seems that the architecture of the city has partially lost its primacy over the establishment of spatial order. Instead, it is confronted with technical developments that override the perceived character of urban or architectural situations.[1]

The supposed importance of historically grown architectural rules for the organization of space seems less prominent than commonly assumed. Rather, the physical manifestation of the city appears as the result of competing systems of order. In fact, the urban environment resembles a montage of unrelated components of our everyday life: The accelerated traveling through space via infrastructural facilities coincides with the fundamental need for privacy, intimacy, and silence (fig. 2). Formerly distant events collapse through the interference of enclosed spaces and the visual representation of distant spaces via digital communication techniques, and the unprecedented availability of images and advertisements (fig. 3), reflection and light profoundly transforms the perception of the urban environment (figs. 9–12). These phenomena have led to a multitude of hybrid spaces and new spatial sequences that challenge a traditional understanding of architecture.

---

1   For an examination of technology and the perception of space, see Virilio 1984: 9–31.

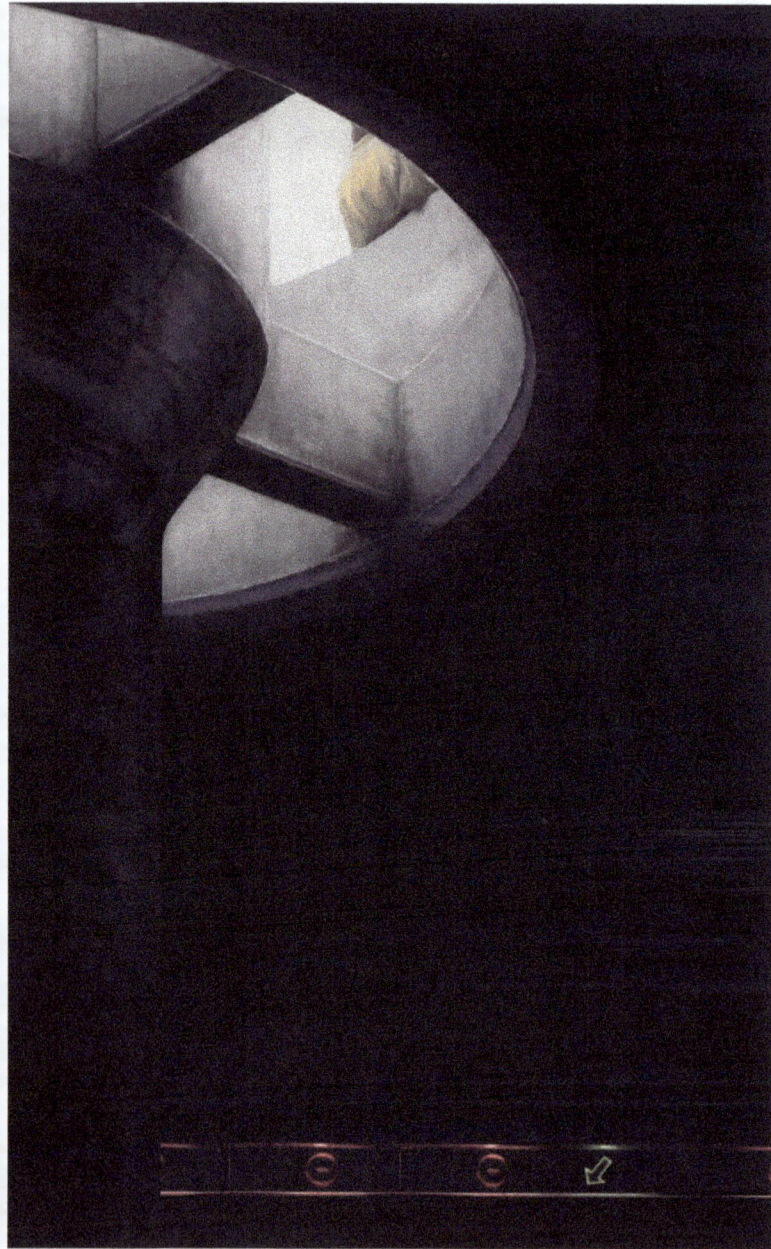

4.
The fluent transition between interior and exterior spaces without any distinct architectural element marking the definitive threshold.
Digitally painted, 410 x 594mm (wings), 495 x 594mm (central panel), 2021.

Particularly in the dense environment of the metropolis, classical distinctions, such as the transition from the exterior of the city to the interior of a building (fig. 4), the legibility of the boundaries between individual buildings, or the division between private and public spheres are called into question or arranged in new ways. Here too, the sheer size of individual developments and the multitude of individual interests negotiated within them contribute to an increased complexity of spatial contexts and the resulting difficulty of assigning them to precise categories. Thus, it is not only the guided movement, which takes place at a variable speed, that has changed the urban space. The development does not stop at the fact that facades are designed for the accelerated perception of the car driver or train passenger. The above mentioned examples are symptomatic of spatial developments that have become deeply inscribed in our everyday lives and are widely accepted because they are often essential to daily life. Despite this acceptance, on closer examination, they express a break with any architectural tradition. Urban planning principles for the unambiguous qualification or aesthetic description of these spaces cannot be applied here, nor can the frequently attempted categorization of basic architectural elements and their assignment of constant qualities for the creation of privacy or publicity. Foucault's observation that »we are in the epoch of simultaneity: we are in the epoch of juxtaposition, the epoch of the near and far, of the side-by-side, of the dispersed« (Foucault 1984: 46), therefore, has the greatest possible relevance and illustrates the complexity of the present-day environment.

Qualities of Space

The awareness of the described ambiguous spatial condition became the basis for the series of paintings *Qualities of Space*. In each of these paintings, contradictions and ambiguities are expressed. In each of them, architectural categories are questioned, and the vague and complex spatial environments that have been accepted as part of the urban environment are brought into focus. This project emerged from the fascination with the fragmented and montaged character of spatial situations within the urban environment. At the same time, the project was driven by interest in the apparent self-evidence for the naturalness with which this conglomerate of spatial articulations of different ways of life, needs and interests are accepted as part of everyday life. It is no longer the shock, triggered by the fragmentation of the cityscape at the end of the 19th century, that sparked this project (Stierli 2018) – it is the detailed consideration of, and the focus on the assembled character of a multifaceted spatial environment that is largely considered an ordinary part of our everyday life.

In this series, painting as a technique of the pictorial representation of architecture was used to gain clarity about the different formulations and questions that arise from the described influences on the architectural environment of the metropolis. Through painting, thoughts were gradually condensed and channeled into depictions of interiors with individual thematic emphases. Thereby, the composition and selection of the individual architectural elements within a painting gained enormous importance and became decisive for their intended allusions and expression.

5.–8.

The passive movement through spaces. Digitally painted, 594 x 420mm, 2021.

9.
Treacherous walls.
Digitally painted, 841 x 594 mm, 2021.

10. *(right)*
Transparencies.
Digitally painted, 841 x 594 mm, 2021.

The individual images do not stand alone. They can be read as a sequence in which the individual architectural representations are related to one another, and a reading direction emerges between the single pieces. This montage of individual images results in a multitude of further readings and imaginary connections; finally, the possibility of using the empty spaces and gaps between the individual images as a narrative element.

Thereby, the images, which consistently reproduce a human visitor's point of view, take up a sequential understanding of architectural perception. Here, spatial perception is understood as a sequence of successive stimuli and impressions of a moving viewer, from which the impression of a building is finally assembled.[2] Analogously, the images can be read as a journey through an imaginary environment. The themes of the individual paintings, such as the intermingling of public and private, physical space and digital image or the transition between infrastructure and architectural interior combine to shed light on the ambiguous nature of the built environment itself.

---

2 For further readings on the mentioned perception of architecture, see Eisenstein 1989 [1937–1940]; Le Corbusier 1923; Baudrillard/Nouvel 2000; Murch 2001.

The painted style of the images includes a strong realism. Nevertheless, on closer inspection, they are recognizable as painted representations and accordingly, they play with the contrast between the credibility of realistic representations of space and the fundamental questioning of the depicted situation in figurative painting. The nature of paintings invites us to challenge the credibility of the composition, analyze viewed objects and spaces critically, and thereby build relationships between the individual heterogeneous elements and read the image symbolically. Even executed with much attention to the natural behavior of light and color, paintings expose themselves as interpreted or imagined spaces and compositions.

The works are digitally painted. They were created using a pressure-sensitive stylus and painting software on a tablet, and subsequently found their way into the physical world as prints. This technique was explicitly chosen as a working tool for this project. It incorporates an imitation of analog painting techniques through a set of digital tools that allow the artist to mimic the color mixing of acrylic and oil paint, control the flow of the paint, and reproduce the fineness or dryness of different brushes. Digital painting thus makes it possible to transfer some well-known working techniques from the field of traditional painting and produce results that are very similar to physically painted images.

Despite the possibility of mimicking the behavior of physical paint on a tablet's display, the process of creating these images is profoundly different. The specifics of individual painting media are not represented and working in layers to create richer colors is not necessary anymore. Options for the subsequent adjustment of color, perspective changes, and the combination of painting techniques and three-dimensional working methods also make it possible to copy the image, adapt it, and combine it with other images. The three-dimensionality of paint is reduced to a surface whose thickness is far less than the fraction of a millimeter. The effects of paint's thickness in impasto techniques are possible to identify, but it remains a simplification of the image into a completely two-dimensional work. Besides that, the question of the original version remains unresolved. Digital images exist in an unlimited number of copies, formats, prints, and color variations depending on the respective display, printer, and surface. Each individual version of the image obscures its origin and makes it difficult to identify digitally painted images as prints of actually digitally generated artworks, as scanned, respectively photographed versions of paintings or montages of multiple images. What is expressed here is a mixing of conceptual models and ways of thinking derived from classical painting with actual working methods that are based on completely different mechanisms and schools of thought: it is a collision that manifests itself, for example, in taking up the classical picture format of the triptych (fig. 4) and the following adjustment and alienation of the work created by means of digital image production. It is the continuation of classical painting techniques on the one hand and the knowledge, on the other hand, that the strokes of a stylus merely produce a set of visualized data. In the end, the described technique leads to the emergence of an image whose style references classical painting, although it is in fact only loosely connected to it.

This intermingling is a phenomenon typical of the current time: The ever-increasing mixing of individual disciplines and their overlap with influences from the most disparate fields; the disappearance of uniform processes and traditions separated from one another in favor of branching, hybrid forms, and the mutual influence of traditional cultural practices and digital techniques and environments; the continuation of individual patterns and practices worthy of preservation from the cultural fundus and their simultaneous decontextualization through their insertion into an environment shaped by technology and digitization. These developments result in a multiple ways of seeing one and the same phenomenon, as well as in a complicated classification of environments, phenomena or the genesis of objects. It is this ambiguous state that is embodied in both the content of the images and the technique used for their creation.

11.
studies, pencil, 105x148mm, 2021.

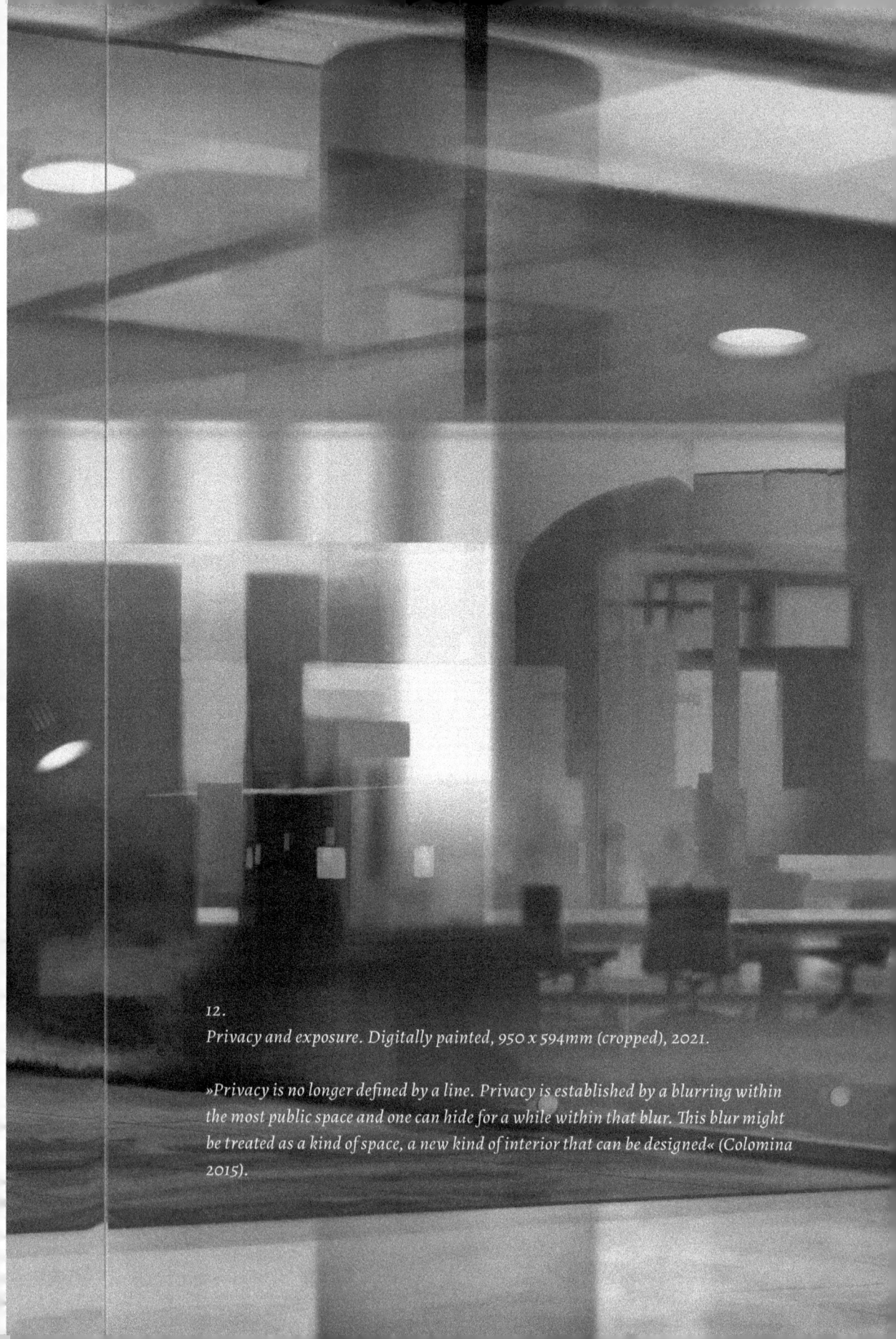

12.
Privacy and exposure. Digitally painted, 950 x 594mm (cropped), 2021.

»Privacy is no longer defined by a line. Privacy is established by a blurring within the most public space and one can hide for a while within that blur. This blur might be treated as a kind of space, a new kind of interior that can be designed« (Colomina 2015).

References

Baudrillard, Jean/Nouvel, Jean (2000): *Les objets singuliers (Singular objects)*, Paris: Calmann-Levy.

Colomina, Beatriz (2015): »unclear visions«, in: *El Croquis 179/180: SANAA Kazuyo Sejima Ryue Nishizawa*, 390–398.

Eisenstein, Sergei M. (1989 [1937–1940]): »Montage and Architecture«, transl. by Michael Glenny, in: *Assemblage 10*, 110–131.

Foucault, Michel (1986): »Of Other Spaces«, transl. by Jay Miskowiec, in: *Diacritics*, Spring, 1986, vol. 16, no. 1, The John Hopkins Press, 22–27.

Le Corbusier (1923): *Vers une architecture.* – English translation by Frederick Etchells: *Towards a New Architecture*, transl. from the 13th French edition, London: John Rodker, 1927, repr. Oxford: Architectural Press, 1989.

Murch, Walter (2001): *In the Blink of an Eye: A Perspective on Film Editing*, Berlin: Alexander Verlag.

Stierli, Martino (2018): *Montage and the Metropolis: Architecture, Modernity, and the Representation of Space*, New Haven/London: Yale University Press.

Virilio, Paul (1984): »La ville surexposée«, in: Paul Virilio (ed.), *L'espace critique (The critical space)*, Paris: Bourgois, 9–31. – English translation: »The Overexposed City«, transl. by Astrid Hustvedt, in: Jonathan Crary et al. (eds.), *Zone 1/2: The Contemporary City*, New York: Urzone, 1986, 14–31.

13. (left)
Sketches and studies, 148x210mm, 2021.

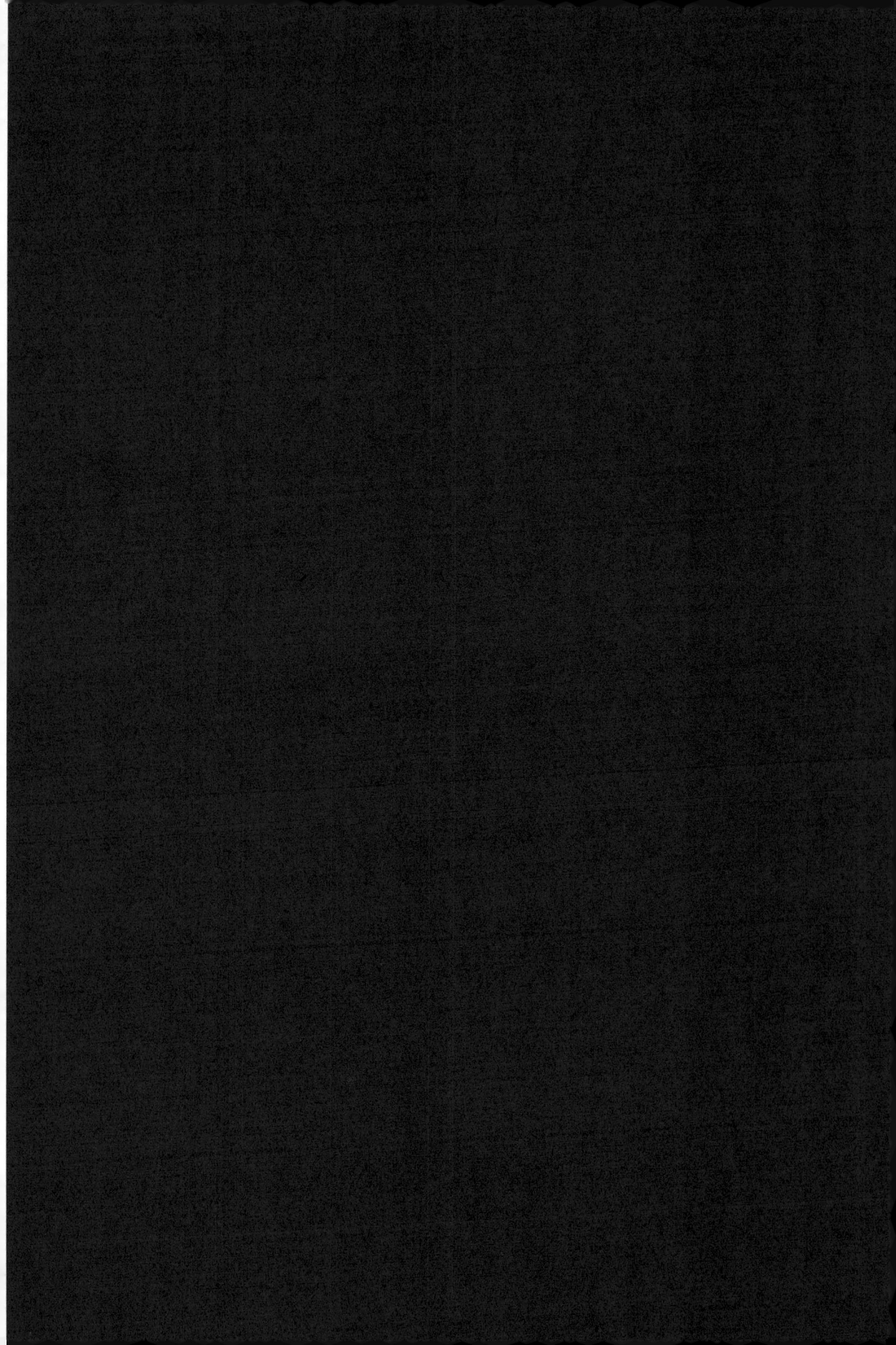

Dimensions. Journal of Architectural Knowledge, 2022-04 ∂
https://doi.org/10.14361/dak-2022-0414

Mind the Gaps
Brutalism, Montage, and Parkour

Charles Engle

Abstract: Parkour is the sport of rapid and efficient movement across the cityscape. Less than 50 years old, parkour matured alongside the internet and handheld recording devices. Combining a *flâneur's dérive* with a daredevil attitude, *traceurs* unlock a hidden ludic stratum of the built environment. By applying Eisenstein's montage theory and Choisy's peripatetic analysis of the Acropolis, parkour's legibility increases dramatically. Eliding the Brutalism of the *IMAX* at Waterloo Station, London and Manpower Gap in Évry, France, a montage of architecture and sport is created. Trespassing and transgressive, parkour is about unrestricted movement and the defying of the planned intent. Pitting architecture, society, moving bodies, and film against each other, sites and runs must be montaged to be understood. Dynamically promenaded via chase and body cameras, the mobile viewer transcends quotidian architecture, makes new meaning, and temporarily escapes the strictures of the metropolis.

Keywords: Brutalism; Eisenstein; Montage; Movement; Nomadism; Parkour; Performance; Storror.

Corresponding author: Charles Engle (Independent Scholar, Savannah, GA, USA);
cengle21@student.scad.edu; http://orcid.org/0000-0002-6478-5615

Parkour, Architecture, and Cinema

Parkour or *l'art du déplacement* is the sport of rapid and efficient movement across cityscapes. Parkour comes from the French *parcours* meaning a path or journey. Ines Braune, a professor at Philipps-University Marburg's Department of Arabic Studies, states: »Parkour today is a global subcultural scene that combines street with media practices« (Braune 2021: 175). Eliding a *flâneur's dérive* with a daredevil attitude, *traceurs* (parkour practitioners) physically trace their way through the architectural landscape of the city, the suburb, or the site via dynamic movement. Refusing the authority of walls, street grids, and architectural intent, they make new meaning. Athletic nomads, traceurs perform across the city. They transgress boundaries and norms through their sport. Free movement is always opposed and thus becomes political (de Lange 2019).

Less than 50 years old, parkour matured alongside the internet and handheld recording devices. The critical strategy of parkour is montage and parallels what Yve-Alain Bois said: »It may also be the path followed by the mind across a multiplicity of phenomena, far apart in time and space, gathered in a certain sequence into a single meaningful concept« (Eisenstein 1989 [1937–1940]: 116). Parkour documentaries utilize this formulation to create their meaning. Making architecture, the body, and politics confront each other in space, parkour takes the fragments from their collision and fuses them together to create new meaning (Ortuzar 2009).

Witnessing a *traceur* in action often leaves one shocked and in disbelief. What was once a normal streetscape or urban feature suddenly becomes a performance site. Charismatic individuals and teams such as Storror have taken advantage of new media to raise their profiles. Storror alone has over 7.54 million followers on YouTube and more than 800 million views (Storror 2022). Filming in locations in numerous countries and continents, the group's documentary style is casual, compelling, and self-shot (Storror 2021). Whether the footage comes from the roofs of Hong Kong, the favelas of Brazil, the streets of Europe, or elsewhere, these documentaries reveal nomadic politics and a defiant attitude toward the mundane expectation of movement.

Methodology

This article examines the *IMAX* at Waterloo Station, London and Manpower Gap in Évry, France (figs. 1–4). The *IMAX* is a large set of Brutalist stairs and ramps while Manpower Gap has been built in the same style, but it is a void between a winder staircase and a lower roof.

Applied to these sites is the montage theory of Soviet filmmaker Sergei Eisenstein (1898–1948) and the peripatetic analysis of the Acropolis by French architectural historian Auguste Choisy (1841–1909). This present study examines how architecture, montage, and sport overlap and shine light on an area that has received little scholarly attention. Parkour is a lens through which the city may be observed to find a realm of performance, protest, and play that is otherwise hidden.

Michel Foucault contended that architecture was not an object but a process; that architecture was not a thing but a flow, and not an abstract idea but a lived thought (Foucault 1972). Parkour honors this insight by viewing architecture as a process for challenging the city, exploring it, and making new meaning therein. When done well, a *traceur* seems to effortlessly flow through the built environment. Eisenstein's montage theory is the mental and cinematic method through which parkour runs are stitched together, while Choisy's peripatetic promenading of architectural space represents the physical act of solving the challenges of the built environment.

Bois cites Swiss-German artist, Paul Klee (1879–1940) who said: »The eye must ›graze‹ over the surface, sharply grasping portion after portion, to convey them to the brain, which collects and stores the impression« (Klee 1960 [1925]: 33). The *traceur* does this, but with their hands and feet. The Museum of Modern Art's chief curator of architecture and design, Martino Stierli highlights Eisenstein's point who asks »what characterizes the montage and hence its role as cell or movie frame? The collision–the conflict of two opposing pieces« (Stierli 2018: 198). When montaged together along with the collisions, the impressions that arise give parkour documentaries their compelling feel. Depicting the struggle between man and architecture, at times, they become physical metaphors for protest and the state. In so doing, what was once a sport documentary can suddenly become political.

1.

Luke Stones, »The IMAX, Waterloo Station«, London, 2020.
Available at: https://www.youtube.com/watch?v=SCE-vsW03mY (accessed
September 22, 2021). Attribution-Generic 2.0 (CCBY 2.0).

2.

Luke Stones, »The IMAX, Waterloo Station«, London, 2020.
Available at: https://www.youtube.com/watch?v=SCE-vsW03mY (accessed
September 22, 2021). Attribution-Generic 2.0 (CCBY 2.0).

3.

Parkour 59, »Manpower Gap«, Évry, France, 2011.
Available at: https://www.youtube.com/watch?v=vccaxGmyHNo (accessed
November 13, 2021). Attribution 3.0 Unported (CC BY 3.0).

4.

Shane Rounce, »Manpower Gap«, Évry, France, 2013,
Available at: https://www.flickr.com/photos/shanerounce/8678811297 (accessed
November 6, 2021). Attribution-NonCommercial-ShareAlike 2.0 Generic (CC
BY-NC-SA 2.0).

Architecture was traditionally considered from three perspectives: plan, site, and elevation. The fourth mode, preferred by Choisy for its mobility, was axonometry, which freed the immobile »camera« and allowed peripatetic observation to occur. For Eisenstein, mobile viewership permits a cinematic reading of a location and solves the problem that prior absolutist regimes such as the baroque enforced; to wit, static tableaus designed from a single perspective. Concerned with parallax, Bois writes of Eisenstein's investigations into how a scene changes with movement. Always a cinematographic choice, the angle of the shot has positive and negative attributes. Gaps may be widened or narrowed, time and space compressed, or expanded if sped up or slowed down, all of which affect our understanding of the space and the body's passage through it. Parkour inserts the moving body into architecture. Bois writes: »And this concern, in turn, reinscribed a most ›concrete‹ term (the bodily movement of the spectator) into the highly ›abstract‹ field of architecture« (Eisenstein 1989 [1937–1940]: 113). United, architecture and the body form a dyad through which meaning and experience are created.

Explicating Eisenstein's project, Bois describes how the task was to transform architecture »from a passive setting of the action, into a major agent of the plot« (ibid.). This runs contrary to the position held by the French architect Robert Mallet-Stevens (1886–1945), for instance, who saw it as a setting and not as an actor (Stierli 2018). Like an alpinist's documentary, the mountain, or in parkour's case, the architectural feature or site, becomes the antagonist. Since the relationship between site and body is never certain, montage allows the cinematographer to dissect and reconnect movement, space, and time in new ways.

Realizing the cinematic nature of buildings, Eisenstein's insight is that the Acropolis is spatialized and understood through movement. A single immobile spectator cannot take in the entire structure alone. Eisenstein writes: »But if the spectator cannot move, he has to gather in one unique point the elements of that which is dispersed in reality, unseizable to a single gaze« (Eisenstein 1989 [1937–1940]: 111). Jane Rendell contends that when moving through space, the built environment and objects can be so banal as to become invisible (Rendell 2006: 188). It is the *traceur*'s gaze however, which is also the cinematographer's gaze, which enables the performativity of a site to emerge. To enable this cinematic aspect, the *traceur* cameramen must create new first impressions. Shocking the viewer into reevaluating and reseeing a site in a new way is what allows the architecture to acquire agency and oppose the *traceur*.

Choisy said that the »creation of a favorable first impression was evidently the constant concern of Greek architects« (Eisenstein 1989 [1937–1940]: 120). To achieve this required polyfocality and peripatetic movement through space, John Miliadis, a late director of the Acropolis Museum, wrote that: »The Acropolis, in short, was turned inwards upon itself, and the buildings were related to each other and to this enclosed site, with no relation to the world of nature outside« (Miliadis 1960: 10f). A montage reading of the Acropolis displays the same logic that is found in parkour documentaries. Self-contained, the documentary creates an internal structure that allows the site to be juxtaposed or fragmented with others in order to create a new gestalt experience.

Parkour is perhaps one of the best expressions of Choisy and Eisenstein's combined theories. The latter remarked that »Cinematographic montage is, too, a means to ›link‹ in one point–the screen–various elements (fragments) of a phenomenon filmed in diverse dimensions, from diverse points of views and side« (Eisenstein 1989: 111). Linking together the city, society, and the state, traceurs demolish, regenerate, and rehabilitate our assumptions about our surroundings and their meanings.

IMAX and Manpower Gap

At London's Waterloo Station there is the BFI *IMAX* theater. The Waterloo complex is the largest station in the United Kingdom. Some of the earliest footage of traceurs at the *IMAX* shows performances from before 2007 when the site was renovated and its coloring changed from orange to blues and blacks. Located in the middle of a roundabout, the theater is adjacent to the underground tube's entrance to King's College. The entrance is known to traceurs as the *IMAX* after the theater and is one of parkour's most iconic sites.

The *IMAX* features a wide central staircase consisting of three flights of stairs and two medial landings; running alongside it is a ramp. Between the two is a concrete balustrade that meets the inner wall of the ramp. On the other side of the stairs, there is a gap before meeting the upper balustrade that surrounds the entire point of egress to the station. From top to bottom, it is roughly 30-feet tall. Brutalist in design, the *IMAX* has sky-blue raw concrete with darker zones of navy and black. From street level, the entirety of the structure cannot be seen, nor can it be fully seen from the bottom. Often, traceurs make their initial jumps blind to the rest of the site.

The experiential quality of the *IMAX* lies in its location between the theater and the station. As a portal between the transportation systems above and below the ground, the *IMAX* by its very nature supports mobility and transiency. Linked by its name, the site sometimes acts as an impromptu amphitheater next to its larger sibling. A physical nexus, the *IMAX* is a bricolage of architecture and cinema. Readymade and available, traceurs use these architectural elements to structure their movements. From the Victorian King's College to the Brutalist metro design, the setting is haphazard and jumbled, but when montaged and performed on by traceurs, they are able to elide such diversity seamlessly through film. Traveling through historical time is achieved using physical leaps and bounds, while meaning is made through juxtaposition, union, and opposition. In this way, the *IMAX* acts as a heterotopia with negotiable boundaries.

Due to its layout, it is not possible to view *IMAX* across all its dimensions. It must be montaged to be understood. When this is joined with parkour *IMAX's* cinematic quality unfolds. No single frame properly captures the *IMAX* and so, the viewer must stitch them together to render and make sense of the final scene. With action shots, B-roll footage, interstitial reactions, and commentary, it is as Eisenstein writes: »The blow is struck only when the elements are juxtaposed into a sequential image« (Eisenstein 1989 [1937–1940]: 128). This juxtaposition is directly that of the body and the site. What was once an unremarkable piece of urban terrain suddenly becomes a locus for attention.

Stephen Barber, a professor of art, design, and architecture at Kingston College writes that contemporary performance is predominantly an intersection of the city, film, and moving-image media. Performances occur in highly visible areas, interstitial ones, occluded ones, and infiltrated areas, all of which describe parkour's many settings. He asserts that the nexus between film and performance »also entails explorations of vertically oriented transits – upwardly oriented gazing and falls from buildings in vertiginous plummeting through city space« (Barber 2014: 30). It is this sense of plummeting that is expressed in the next site.

Located near the Tribunal Judiciaire in Évry, France, the Manpower Gap is nestled in a mixed residential and commercial area. It is near to where parkour's founder David Belle (b. 1973) trained in the 1980s and 1990s. Growing up in the housing projects of Évry, he constantly interacted with Brutalist architecture. Mega-structural, these buildings created urban canyons, walls, boulders, chimneys, stairs, pillars, and other topologies upon which to play.

Manpower is an interstitial void between the thin perimeter wall of a Brutalist winder staircase roughly 45-feet tall and across a 10-foot gap and 15-foot drop to a rooftop below at 30-feet of elevation. The jump's difficulty comes from requiring a standing leap and an unforgiving trajectory. In the image presented, above the lower roof's right corner, the *traceur* flies toward his landing across this fatal drop. The *traceur's* action would normally never be considered by a designer. Braune remarks that this dialectical relationship »implies new ways in which space is negotiated and appropriated that were not originally intended by city planners and architects« (Braune 2021: 184).

Évry's Brutalist architecture helps to create a multi-level and multi-volume topology. Labyrinthine, the space around the gap follows the same program that Le Corbusier used in his buildings that required inhabitants to actively travel through their architectural space. The surrounding housing has balconies, ledges, terraces, and towers that all blur the line between inside and outside, and is perhaps why Manpower does the same with stairs and roofs. Acting as a place of pilgrimage for daredevil devotees who wish to add the iconic site to their resume, Manpower was montaged by Storror in 2019. The team used more than three shot angles, drone footage, and a mouth-held GoPro to achieve the polyfocality needed to comprehend the movement and action of their attempt (Taylor 2019). Due to the *IMAX* and Manpower requiring more than a single frontal perspective to be fully apprehended, several covering shots must be elided together to generate the mental map. Eisenstein elucidates further upon this: »The calculation of a shot effect is obvious, for there, too, the effect of the first impression from each new, emerging shot is enormous. Equally strong, however, is the calculation on a montage effect, that is, the sequential juxtaposition of those shots« (Eisenstein 1989 [1937–1940]: 120). Shots of the site, the flying body, reactions, and other occurrences montaged from different angles create a unique experience that is otherwise hidden by the architectural program. Expanding beyond these two sites, traceurs will often perform at more than one site. Linked together in documentary, they create a montaged expression of a given city.

Mobility, Politics, Space

Jimena Ortuzar, a visiting postdoctoral fellow at Ryerson University, writes that a run occurs when »parkouristes storm *through* the city, transforming it into a playground where chance, interaction, and imagination, provide countless opportunities to challenge, on one hand, the rigidity of space and, on the other, the precariousness of urban life« (Ortuzar 2009: 56). Scott Budzynski, Professor of Art History at Savannah College of Art and Design, adds to this line of thought by suggesting that creative and subversive experience of urban environments invites chance and uncertainty into the mix (Budzynski 2015: 92). This notion of chance aligns with the earlier *dérive* tradition of groups such as the Letterists and the later Situationist International, which parkour honors. By inviting chaos into the montage, parkour documentarians privilege the anarchic and spontaneous, which often runs counter to the architecturally planned efficiency of urban spaces. Ortuzar argues further that traceurs are artists »skipping over links, substituting totalities with fragments, and omitting entire parts of the city through far-reaching leaps« (Ortuzar 2009: 63). Creating, fragmenting, and omitting are all techniques that permit a montage reading of a site or the city.

Architects, researchers, and scholars contend that by fragmenting and juxtaposing the political situation, traceurs turn non-ludic spaces into stages (Geertman et al. 2016). Traceurs will often opportunistically occupy an area of the city turning it into an unauthorized, momentary, and consciously subversive performance space. Toby Segar, a member of Storror explained why his team was unique: »[We] have the audacity to complete a task or project regardless of what the norm or current trend may be, regardless of authority, effort, or potentially controversial implications« (Storror 2022). Anarchic and nomadic, traceurs refuse the status quo suggested by their surrounding architecture.

Budzynski asserts »that public space is for use rather than exchange, that one should use the public realm regardless of who one is or what one owns, and that the way we use public space is an essential factor of who we are« (Budzynski 2015: 92). Nomadic traceurs refute claims of spatial ownership and instead argue for temporary and spontaneous claims of utilization. In this way, traceurs develop their identities and through them become political. Stierli notes that this accords with Eisenstein's belief that montaged media was a channel for politically engaging and educating the masses, which traceurs do through their videos (Stierli 2018). Both parkour and

Choisy's analysis can be unified through Stierli's insight that »Montage is of necessity political – as is public space, of which the Acropolis is the ultimate prototype« (Stierli 2018: 198). Parkour has even been performed on the Acropolis, which of course was controversial in and of itself (The Moscow Times 2014).

Brutalism and Parkour

The origins of parkour can be found in the widespread creation of low-cost housing blocks in post-war Europe and with Le Corbusier's *Unité d'Habitation* beginning in the 1940s. He inverted the city with his design and gave the building interior streets while simultaneously allowing access to the outside. Atop the building was a nursery where children interacted with its architecture and learned to play. Modeled after an ocean liner, the Unité d'Habitation became an urban ark. In such an arrangement, the roof becomes the deck and the logical place to play.

Brutalist buildings were often made to human scale. Le Corbusier's *Unité d'Habitation* was built around his concept of the »Modulor Man«. He said that it was »Made for men, it is made to the human scale« (Frearson 2014). Using a grid-based measurement system, it is akin to Da Vinci's *L'uomo vitruviano*, as both use the human body as a ruler. Due to this, Brutalist buildings have features such as gaps, levels, ramps, and stairs that facilitate parkour activities. At the *IMAX*, it is the spacing between upper and medial rails and the gaps between that entice traceurs to test their skills. Manpower instead relies on the penetrability of Brutalist architecture.

Le Corbusier and Eisenstein both respected each other's work and the former said of the latter: »Architecture and the cinema are the only two arts of our time. In my own work I seem to think as Eisenstein does in his films ... His films resemble closely what I am striving to do in my own work« (Stierli 2018: 183). The use of movement, polyfocality, and peripatetic motion all occur in both of their works. Eisenstein identified how movement can change the look, feel, and sense of a scene, and architecture that encourages this tendency becomes naturally cinematic.

Helping to create the Brutalist urban fabric of post-war Britain were the British architects Allison Smithson (1928–1993) and Peter Smithson (1923–2003) who in 1953 coined the term »New Brutalism« and formalized a trend long in the making. Reynar Banham (1922–1988) gave three requirements for

New Brutalism: the clear exhibition of structure; the valuation of materials »as found«, and memorability as an image (McCleod/Churly 2018: 6). This last criterion is especially relevant to the cinematic quality valued by Eisenstein. The Smithsons worked within the Congrès internationaux d'architecture moderne (CIAM) as they continued down the trail that Le Corbusier had blazed. Working on projects such as social housing and institutional buildings, they saw a need to rehabilitate ruined parts of the city (Smithson & Smithson 1957).

Using what was available, Brutalist architects eschewed ornamentation and relied on the materials to speak for them. From architect Owen Luder, »we never set out to design Brutalist buildings. We designed them in concrete because that's what was there. Bear in mind it was the sixties, it was difficult to get steel, it was still rationed« (Mairs 2014). Out of this constraint, the varied topologies and geologies of Brutalism appeared.

Returning to France, the *banlieus* of Paris were where parkour originated with Belle, and they were a reaction to the overcrowding found in the capital. Évry, one of five new towns that was meant to absorb Paris' growing population is where Manpower is located. The suburb possesses many interesting structures such as the nearby Brutalist PMI Pyramides. Lifted from *parcours du combatant*, a French military training regimen devised by Georges Hérbert (1875–1957), parkour was influenced early on by mountaineering (Ameel/Tani 2012). In Évry, a large *béton brut* climbing wall by Hungarian sculptor, Pierre Székely (1923–2001) was erected in 1970 (Angel 2016). Devoid of natural cliffs and mountains, the early traceurs instead realized that their housing areas contained artificial geological features.

Julie Angel, a British filmmaker writes about the suburb, »the striking, repetitive and varied angular geometries created buildings that looked like enormous terraced blocks or stepping stones waiting for mystical giants to cross. The spaces were new ideas reminiscent of the Brutalist architectural philosophy« (ibid.: 17). Eliding with a youthful population, the muscular volumes created »walkways and passages that didn't always connect and places that could often be seen but not easily found or accessed by conventional means« (ibid.). This type of architecture immediately calls for a montage sensibility and a peripatetic viewer.

By the time parkour appeared, the housing estates had already begun to erode both socially and structurally. Brutalist housing was meant to help transition communities and urban areas from ruin and poverty to solid, dense, and deeply permanent structures of prosperity (McCleod/

Churly 2018). Through industrial-scale manufacturing and prefabrication, Brutalism was seen as a way forward. It created buildings for tomorrow with a new progressive ethic through the expressive use of concrete, such as the Robin Hood Gardens by the Smithsons in London which was completed in 1972. It would later be demolished between 2017 and 2019, and be a place where Storror would perform. Commonly featured in parkour documentaries, housing projects form a nexus between architecture and urban youth. Close to home, these areas are often the first places to be explored.

Robin Hood Gardens was meant to be an ideal community that challenged previous norms. Post-war housing estates were meant to shelter communities from the degradations of the city such as noise, traffic, and vandalism. The Smithsons intended their housing project to have »streets in

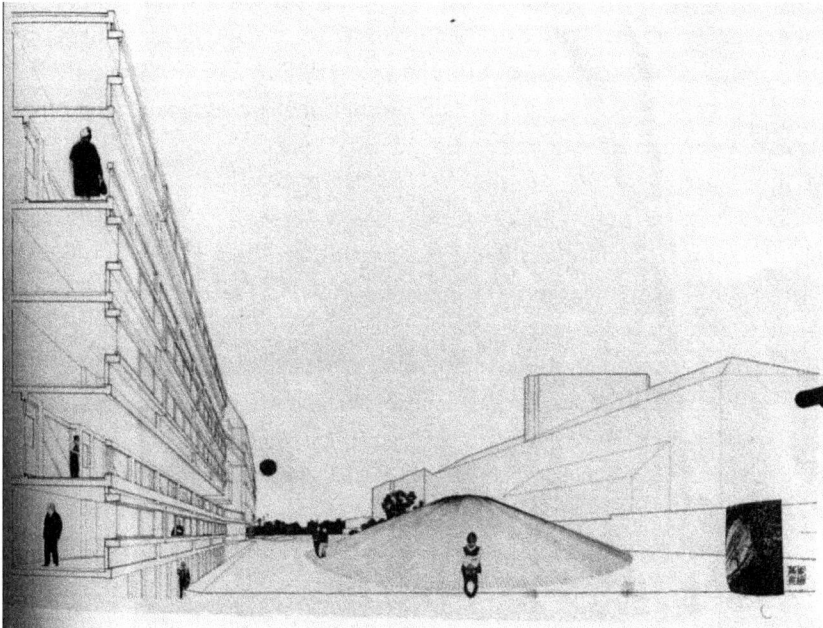

5.
The Alison and Peter Smithson Archive: Manisty Street, Tower Hamlets, 1963.
Courtesy of the Frances Loeb Library, Harvard University Graduate School of Design.

the sky« and a sheltered courtyard intended for play which was made from the rubble of the previous site (fig. 5).

Poorly examined by scholars, this ludic element was intentionally emplaced into the plan of the estate. However, what parkour has done with such sites is to extend the ludic realm into the buildings themselves. The multi-level, multi-volume nature of Brutalist structures and their permeability makes them ideal places for traceurs to train.

Despite their intentions, the Smithsons' vision was quickly upended. Christopher and Olivia Turner remarked that »the architects were blamed for the high crime rate in the complex« and that the Smithsons »were shocked at the speed with which this happened« (Ricci 2018). Although well-intentioned, the current imaginary of these places is as David Pettersen describes: »bleak housing projects, poverty, urban blight, immigrants, and riots, and social unrest« (Pettersen 2014: 26). Traceurs however often see them as romantic places with cinematic qualities. They favor this terrain for its counter-cultural and political identities. The area's undesirability is often a benefit as it often allows the traceurs' activities to go unnoticed.

In a short video produced by Storror, Thamesmead Estate (partially demolished in 2020), is used as a ludic space. In its current form, the estate is a far cry from its original inception as a »town of tomorrow« (Storror 2020).

Living at Thamesmead (1974) was a promotional piece meant to promote the area's social, recreational, and residential spaces (London Metropolitan Archive 2012).

The estate's Brutalist architecture has now deteriorated and in parts has even become urban blight. Repeated with similar effect in other countries, Europe still has many deteriorating mass-housing estates, which traceurs often explore and train on.

Housing projects can often become proxies for the state. When used politically, parkour documentaries and performances can bring positive or negative attention to specific areas. In this way, sport becomes a vehicle for activism and the parkour documentary its evidence while *traceurs* argue their case. Iain Borden's observations about skateboarders can be applied to parkour. Skateboarders for instance, show an aesthetic sensitivity to their surroundings, which can be extended to traceurs who have a penchant for performing in abandoned places, derelict spaces, and urban ruins (Borden 2001). Inspiring and unique architectural features urge traceurs to improvise in order to reconfigure the cityscape. In doing so, Borden argues that such transformations are subversive because they bring the normally banal built environment into sharp focus.

As an actor that participates in the parkour documentary, architecture is more than material and form. Embedded in the brick and concrete of the city are the laws of the state. Rules govern the usage of sites, access to them, and how they are maintained or condemned. Parkour regenerates eroding Brutalist structures by rehabilitating them. Turned into places of excitement, performance, and sport, these sites are reclaimed by traceurs. Temporarily rejuvenated, such sites are lifted out of their necropolitan states and are transformed into ludic zones. Actively seeking out such blight in 2019, Storror visited Europe's least visited country, Moldova, where some of its failed housing projects suddenly became host to a team of world-class athletes (Taylor 2019).

Parkour in Film

Peter Chadwick, an art director who has closely examined Brutalist architecture notes its cinematic quality. Not only limited to housing areas, traceurs favor multi-story parking garages which they descend in bravura style.

6.

Gordon Barnes: Gateshead Trinity Square Carpark, London, 2008.

Preempting the filmography of parkour are scenes such as in *Get Carter* (1971), which used Trinity Square carpark in London (fig. 6).

With numerous levels, ramps, and walkways, montaging the structure creates a complex mental topography of polyfocal shots as different characters race through different levels and sections of the structure (Chadwick 2016). Unfortunately, these structures have often suffered over the years and many Brutalist sites have fallen into disrepair or have been demolished. The architect of the car park, Owen Luder, lamented this fact in a documentary, »in the sixties my buildings were awarded, in the seventies they were applauded, in the eighties they were questioned, in the nineties they were ridiculed, and when we get through to 2000 the ones I like most are the ones that have been demolished« (Mairs 2014).

In the 2000s, documentaries such as *Jump London* (2003) and *Jump Britain* (2006) helped to raise parkour's visibility (Angel 2016). French director, Luc Besson, deployed it in several of his films. Kaspar Schröder's *My Playground* (2009) is an important work due to its inclusion not only of traceurs and their performances, but also because of the presentation of interviews with architects, politicians, planners, and theorists that give nuance and color to the debate surrounding parkour and the use of space. Storror has appeared in Michael Bay's *6 Underground* (2019) while other traceurs have performed in many other films. Parkour acts as a physical magic trick that perhaps more than any other sport excels at exhibiting architecture as drama.

This was not always the case, however. Early parkour documentaries were not the slick productions that they are today. Drew Taylor of Storror explains how early parkour documentaries were made: »At that time there was a standard formula for making parkour videos. Every season the best training-clips would be uploaded into a montage with a hip-hop beat. That's how everyone did it, long serious logs of training«. However, unwilling to be constrained by a standardized format, the Cave brothers of Storror chose to »break the mould« and changed to a new documentary style that was as much a sport as a lifestyle vlog (Storror 2020). Since David Belle, and now Storror, traceurs are constantly honing their craft both athletically and cinematographically, all the while seeking out new architecture.

Conclusion

Cities are often focused on optimizing the efficient flow of goods and people, and concentrated around hierarchies of wealth and institutional power. Through unrestricted physical movement that equalizes topography, the orderliness of the city is broken in anarchic fashion as *traceurs*, spectators, and the built environment are cast into new roles of activity and meaning. This is captured in parkour documentaries and is perhaps why millions find them so compelling. As a nexus, parkour, and its ability to expand the ludic dimensionality of the built environment requires additional study so that future architects and cinematographers may see the city just as the *traceur* does.

References

Ameel, Lieven/Tani, Sirpa (2012): »Parkour: Creating Loose Spaces?«, in: *Geografiska Annaler. Series B, Human Geography 94, no. 1*, 17–30.

Angel, Julie (2016): *Breaking the Jump: The Secret Story of Parkour's High Flying Rebellion*, London: Aurum Press.

Barber, Stephen (2014): »Performance's Elsewheres: Rooftops, Courtyards, Subterranean Spaces«, in: *Performance Projections: Film and the Body in Action*, London: Reaktion Books Ltd., 28–99

Borden, Iain (2001): *Skateboarding, Space and the City: Architecture and the Body*, New York: Bloomsbury Academic.

Braune, Ines (2021): »Body-Space-Relation in Parkour: Street Practices and Visual Representations«, in: Alena Strohmaier/ Angela Krewani (eds.): *Media and Mapping Practices in the Middle East and North Africa*, Amsterdam: Amsterdam University Press, 175–199.

Budzynski, Scott J. (2015): »Modes of Spatial Exploration in Berlin«, in: *Street Art & Urban Creativity Scientific Journal: Places and Non Places, vol. 1, no. 2*, 89–98, http://www.urbancreativity.org/uploads/1/0/7/2/10727553/journal2015_v1_n2_web_final_upt1.pdf, accessed Oktober 18, 2022.

Chadwick, Peter (2016): *This Brutal World*, London: Phaidon Press Ltd.

de Lange, Michiel (2019): »The playful city: Citizens making the smart city«, in: René Glas/Sybille Lammes/ Michiel de Lange et al. (eds.), *The Playful Citizen: Civic Engagement in a Mediatized Culture*, Amsterdam: Amsterdam University Press, 349–369.

Eisenstein, Sergei M. (1989 [1937–1940]): »Montage and Architecture«, transl. by Michael Glenny, in: *Assemblage 10*, 110–131.

Foucault, Michel (1972): *The Archaeology of Knowledge and the Discourse on Language*, transl. by A. M. Sheridan Smith, New York: Pantheon Books.

Frearson, Amy (2014): »Brutalist buildings: Unité d'Habitation, Marseille by Le Corbusier«, September 15, 2014, https://www.dezeen.com/2014/09/15/le-corbusier-unite-d-habitation-cite-radieuse-marseille-brutalist-architecture/, accessed June 5, 2022.

Geertman, Stephanie/Labbé, Danielle/Boudreau, Julie-Anne/Jacques, Olivier (2016): »Youth-Driven Tactics of Public Space Appropriation in Hanoi: The Case of Skateboarding and Parkour«, in: *Pacific Affairs*, vol. 89, no. 3, 591–611.

Klee, Paul (1960 [1925]): *Pedagogical Sketchbook*, transl. by Sibyl Moholy-Nagy, New York: F. A. Praeger.

London Metropolitan Archives (2012): »Living at the Thamesmead, 1974«, August 13, 2012, https://www.youtube.com/watch?v=NtqX9PJv-Nk, accessed October 28, 2021.

Mairs, Jessica (2014): »Brutalist buildings: Trinity Square car park by Owen Luder«, September 14, 2014, https://www.dezeen.com/2014/09/14/brutalist-buildings-trinity-square-get-carter-car-park-owen-luder/, accessed June 4, 2022.

MANPOWER (2019): »Most ICONIC roof gap in Parkour history«, December 12, 2019, https://www.youtube.com/watch?v=YCaWtrrm9Uk&t=446s, accessed November 3, 2021.

McCleod, Virginia/Churly, Clare (eds.) (2018): *Atlas of Brutalist Architecture*. London: Phaidon Press.

Miliadis, John (1960): *The Acropolis*. Athens: Pechlivanidis & Co. Ltd.

Ortuzar, Jimena (2009): »Parkour or *l'art du déplacement*: A Kinetic Urban Utopia«, in: TDR/*The Drama Review*, vol. 53, no. 3, 54–66.

Pettersen, David (2014): »American Genre Film in the French Banlieue: Luc Besson and Parkour«, in: *Cinema Journal 53, no. 3*, 26–51

Rendell, Jane (2006): *Art and Architecture: A Place Between*, London: I.B. Tauris & Co. Ltd.

Ricci, Giulia (2018): »Robin Hood Gardens is a lesson for futur cities«, October 16, 2018, https://www.domusweb.it/en/speciali/domus-paper/2018/robin-hood-gardens-is-a-lesson-for-future-cities.html, accessed June 8, 2022.

Smithson, Alison/Smithson, Peter (1957): »Thoughts in Progress: The New Brutalism«, in: *Architectural Design*, vol. 27, no. 4, 111–113.

Stierli, Martino (2018): *Montage and the Metropolis: Architecture, Modernity, and the Representation of Space*. New Haven: Yale University Press.

STORROR (2021): »Meet The Team«, https://www.storror.com/about/, accessed November 3, 2021.

STORROR (2021): »Most SCARY Parkour move EVER!«, May 3, 2021, https://www.youtube.com/watch?v=m-2mBs5dbNI, accessed November 6, 2021.

Storror Youtube Channel. 2022. https://www.youtube.com/c/STORROR (accessed August 14, 2022).

STORROR (2020): »What does STORROR mean?«, October 1, 2020, https://www.storror.com/blog/what-does-storror-mean/, accessed November 2, 2021.

Taylor, Drew (2019): »Europe's Least Visited Country«, October 10, 2019, https://www.storror.com/blog/europes-least-visited-country/, accessed October 22, 2022.

The Moscow Times (2014): »Russian Parkour Fans Damage Athens' Acropolis«, October 7, 2014, https://www.themoscowtimes.com/2014/10/07/russian-parkour-fans-damage-athens-acropolis-a40138, accessed November 12, 2021.

Contributors

Erieta Attali (Dr.)

has devoted herself to the interplay between architecture & landscape for the past thirty years. Through her pioneering work, she has forged a new path in architectural photography where content and context are inverted.

Her photography explores how extreme conditions and challenging terrains cause humanity to reorient and recenter itself through architectural responses. Her unconventional photography is based on a working method drawn from her experience in archaeology and fine art photography. Her current research is focused on urban landscapes in Paris and Singapore as well as the Jewish Architecture Heritage in Thessaloniki. She recently won the German Photo Book Award 19|20 with her photographic monograph *Periphery | Archaeology of Light* published by Hatje Cantz and her photographs have been exhibited in important museums around the world. Attali is a research scholar at Paris 1 Panthéon-Sorbonne and a Visiting Professor at the National University in Singapore.

Stefana Dilova

grew up in Sofia, Bulgaria and Sendai, Japan. Her projects explore the poetic and atmospheric qualities of everyday spaces, as well as the stories of their inhabitants, through formats such as film, photography and installation. Her work *The Poetics of Home* was first shown in the *Scope BLN Art Space* as part of a solo exhibition that took place in the summer of 2021. Dilova holds a B.Sc. in Architecture from the Technical University Berlin and a M.A. in Architecture from the University of Arts Berlin. She lives and works in Berlin. *www.stefanadilova.com*

Charles Engle

is a graduate student at Savannah College of Art and Design (SCAD) for Art History with a focus on Russian art and architecture. His undergraduate degree was from Illinois State University in Anthropology and a certificate from Nagoya Gakuin Daigaku in Japanese Studies. Then he taught English and science in Korea before accepting services into the U.S. Peace Corps as an education volunteer in Petropavl, Kazakhstan. There, he worked as an English teacher and as a translator for its *Regional Folk History Museum*. Now, he is writing on the art of the Space Race. His thesis will be on Russian expedition painters such as Nikolai Roerich.

Nils Fröhling

studied architecture at the University of Stuttgart and the Technical University of Munich and works as an architect and painter in Munich. His personal work and research focus on the translation of space into two-dimensional images and the analogies, connections and gaps between architecture and its pictorial and filmic representation. This interest is expressed through his painted works, written projects and collaborations in the fields of stage design and production design for feature film productions. Fröhling teaches the seminar *Scenography* at the Technical University of Munich. This course explicitly addresses the conveyance of spatial perception through pictorial and cinematic means. (In collaboration with the University of Television and Film Munich, HFF). *www.nils-froehling.com*

Julian Franke

currently holds a position as research assistant at the Competence Center Typology and Planning at the Lucerne University of Applied Sciences and Arts, researching in projects on the Anthropocene, building culture, and urban development. He completed degrees in architecture at the Münster School of Architecture and the Technical University Berlin as well as in philosophy at the Technical University Berlin with a scholarship at University College Cork, Ireland. Franke worked as an architect in several architecture offices in Berlin and Zurich. Since 2022 he is a PhD student at the Department of Architecture Theory at Technical University Berlin. His recently published book *Erfahrungswelten. Wahrnehmung und Imagination der Architektur (Worlds of Experience. Perception and Imagination of Architecture)* (transcript 2020) examines the complex levels of perception and the importance of the immaterial in architecture. His work in practice and theory focuses on topics at the intersections of architecture philosophy, epistemology, aesthetics and future ethics.

Katrine Majlund Jensen

is a cultural worker and architectural heritage researcher based in Berlin. She holds a B.A. in Aesthetics and Culture from Aarhus University and Vrije Universiteit, Amsterdam. She holds a Master's degree in World Heritage Studies from BTU Cottbus and has been part of the Young Professionals *ICOMOS ISC20C* Mentoring program and been the recipient of the Women's Advancement Initiative scholarship, BTU Cottbus. She was recipient and project coordinator of European Commission Funding and Gwaertler Stiftung for the project Contemporary uses of Listed Buildings, CineEast Short Film Festival Berlin, Kühlhaus Berlin. Her museum work counts among others the exhibition *Neolitische Kindheit, ca. 1930* at *Haus der Kulturen der Welt* as well as work at AROS Aarhus Art Museum. She is currently a PhD Candidate at the DFG (German Research Fund) Research Training Group 1913, *Cultural and technological significance of historic buildings* at BTU Cottbus.

Ulrike Kuch (Dr.)

is a research associate at the chair of Theory and History of Modern Architecture, Faculty of Architecture and Urbanism, and Co-Director of the *Bauhaus-Institut für Geschichte und Theorie der Architektur und Planung* at Bauhaus-University Weimar, Germany. Ulrike earned her doctorate with an transdisciplinary dissertation on Stairs on Film from the Faculty of Media in Weimar. She studied architecture at Bauhaus-Universität, Technical University Helsinki / Finland, University of Arts and Technical University / Berlin. Her fields of research include phenomenology and architecture; architecture and the image and global history of architecture. Recently Ulrike edited *Das Diaphane. Architektur und ihre Bildlichkeit* (transcript 2020) which explores aspects of a mediality of architecture.

Sandra Meireis (Dr.)

is an architecture scholar and author. She lives in Berlin and has been teaching architectural history and theory at various universities since 2010: State Academy of Fine Arts Stuttgart, University of Stuttgart, Technical University of Berlin, University of Applied Sciences Stuttgart and University of Kassel. She did her doctorate at the Chair of Architectural Theory at the Technical University Berlin (2020) and currently holds a position as interim professor for Architecture and Design History / Architecture Theory at the State Academy of Fine Arts Stuttgart, she is board member of the *Netzwerk Architekturwissenschaft e.V.* and associate member of the Association of German Architects (BDA). Her book *Mikro-Utopien der Architektur* (*Architectural Micro-Utopias*) (transcript 2021) examines the recent return of utopian thought in the field of architecture. Her research focuses on the history and theory of architecture and urban design, with topics at the intersection of philosophy of history, cultural and political studies, and aesthetics.

Achim Reese (Dr.)

studied architecture at RWTH Aachen and at the Vienna Academy of Fine Arts, before working as editorial staff for the architectural journal *ARCH+* and the online magazine *Baunetz*. As a fellow at the Kunsthistorisches Institut in Florenz – Max-Planck-Institut, he prepared the dissertation *Orte für das Selbst. Die Architektur Charles W. Moores und ihr gesellschaftspolitischer Anspruch*, supervised by Angelika Schnell and Volker Welker, which was completed in 2021. Since October 2022, Achim Reese has been teaching architectural history and theory at the Technical University of Munich.

Taiyo Onorato & Nico Krebs

have been working together as an artist duo since they met in Zurich University of the Arts in 2003. Their diverse projects are evolving around photography, also involving sculpture, installation, film and book publishing. Their work has been shown internationally in many galleries and institutions, among them solo shows in MoMA PS1 NYC, Kunsthalle Mainz, Foam Amsterdam, Fotomuseum Winterthur, Kunsthaus Aarau, CAC Cincinnati, Swiss Institute NY, LeBal Paris and KINDL Centre for Contemporary Art, Berlin. They published several artist books, among them *The Great Unreal* and *Continental Drift* and *Future Memories*. They regularly hold workshops and teach at many acadamies and Universities around Europe. They live and work between Slovakia, Greece and Switzerland.

Max Treiber

studied architecture at the Münster School of Architecture and the Technical University Berlin. He has been working in several architecture offices in Tokyo, Zurich, and Berlin and lecturing in the field of architectural theory and history at Bochum University of Applied Sciences. Since September 2019 he is a research assistant supervising the students of the first academic year, the Master's Thesis as well as the Seminars *Realmontage*. Since 2020, he has been investigating in the ongoing doctoral thesis *Architectural Montage – Scenarios of Everyday Spaces* the connection between space and image using the example of a body of work by the Italian photographer Luigi Ghirri. In the same year he became a member of the Bavarian Chamber of Architects. Since then he has been working as an independent architect on various projects in Munich and the surrounding area.

Architektur und Design

Pierre Smolarski
Designrhetorik
Zur Theorie wirkungsvollen Designs

2022, 416 S., kart.,
134 SW-Abbildungen, durchgängig zweifarbig
29,00 € (DE), 978-3-8376-5933-7
E-Book: kostenlos erhältlich als Open-Access-Publikation
PDF: ISBN 978-3-8394-5933-1

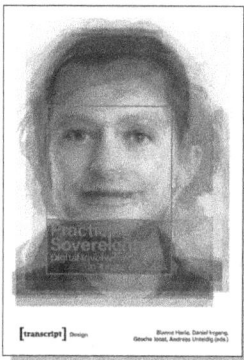

Bianca Herlo, Daniel Irrgang,
Gesche Joost, Andreas Unteidig (eds.)
Practicing Sovereignty
Digital Involvement in Times of Crises

2022, 430 p., pb., col. ill.
35,00 € (DE), 978-3-8376-5760-9
E-Book: available as free open access publication
PDF: ISBN 978-3-8394-5760-3

Christoph Rodatz, Pierre Smolarski (Hg.)
Wie können wir den Schaden maximieren?
Gestaltung trotz Komplexität.
Beiträge zu einem Public Interest Design

2021, 234 S., kart.
29,00 € (DE), 978-3-8376-5784-5
E-Book: kostenlos erhältlich als Open-Access-Publikation
PDF: ISBN 978-3-8394-5784-9

**Leseproben, weitere Informationen und Bestellmöglichkeiten
finden Sie unter www.transcript-verlag.de**

Architektur und Design

Tim Kammasch (Hg.)
Betrachtungen der Architektur
Versuche in Ekphrasis

2020, 326 S., kart., 63 SW-Abbildungen
30,00 € (DE), 978-3-8376-4994-9
E-Book:
PDF: 29,99 € (DE), ISBN 978-3-8394-4994-3

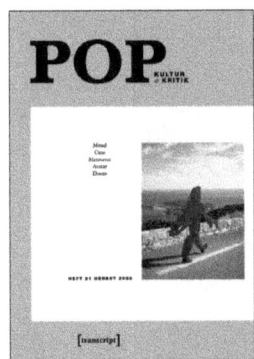

Thomas Hecken, Moritz Baßler, Elena Beregow,
Robin Curtis, Heinz Drügh, Mascha Jacobs,
Annekathrin Kohout, Nicolas Pethes, Miriam Zeh (Hg.)
POP
Kultur und Kritik (Jg. 11, 2/2022)

2022, 180 S., kart.
16,80 € (DE), 978-3-8376-5897-2
E-Book:
PDF: 16,80 € (DE), ISBN 978-3-8394-5897-6

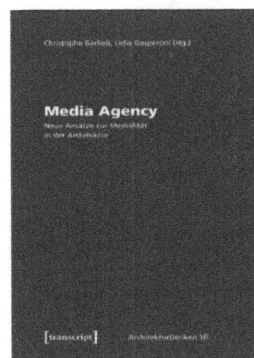

Christophe Barlieb, Lidia Gasperoni (Hg.)
Media Agency –
Neue Ansätze zur Medialität in der Architektur

2020, 224 S., Klappbroschur, 67 SW-Abbildungen
29,99 € (DE), 978-3-8376-4874-4
E-Book: kostenlos erhältlich als Open-Access-Publikation
PDF: ISBN 978-3-8394-4874-8

GPSR Authorized Representative: Easy Access System Europe, Mustamäe tee
50, 10621 Tallinn, Estonia, gpsr.requests@easproject.com